PENTECOSTAL CATHOLICS

PENTECOSTAL CATHOLICS

Edited by
Robert Heyer

PAULIST PRESS
New York / Paramus / Toronto

The articles in this book originally appeared in the Nov./Dec. 1974 issue of *New Catholic World*.

Art and Design: Gloria Ortiz

Library of Congress
Catalog Card Number: 75-10114

ISBN: 0-8091-1879-3

Published by Paulist Press
Editorial Office: 1865 Broadway, N.Y., N.Y. 10023
Business Office: 400 Sette Drive, Paramus, N.J. 07652

Printed and bound in the United States of America

CONTENTS

HOW IT LOOKS TO A SOCIAL SCIENTIST

Joseph H. Fichter

The flourishing and ever-expanding charismatic renewal took the American Catholic Church by surprise. Catholic Pentecostals are serene in the conviction that it is God who "springs" the surprise. With simple faith in the Holy Spirit they agree with Cardinal Suenens who considers this "another instance where God chooses to work in a way that we humans would never have anticipated or chosen." The fact that this eminent European prelate came over to the United States to "learn about" Catholic Pentecostalism is in itself extraordinary. After all, the typical European critic looks on America as

Joseph Fichter, S.J., who teaches sociology at Loyola University in New Orleans, has contributed to this magazine in both its 50th and 75th issues. His latest book, *The Catholic Cult of the Paraclete,* will be published by Sheed and Ward.

the most materialistic, sensate and secular nation in the world—hardly the kind of society to generate a deeply spiritual and devotional movement.

Counter-Culture Ideology

Much has been said and written about this post-Christian age, the decline of religiosity, and the dissolution of spiritual values in Western civilization, with America leading the way. James Hitchcock soberly observed that "there is an obvious spiritual malaise affecting both religious and laymen" in the Catholic Church. Even Andrew Greeley, as recently as 1973, elicited from his research data a somber prediction on the "collapse" of American Catholicism. Yet, out of the heartland of affluent, technological, success-oriented America there has emerged a religious revival that goes counter to contemporary behavioral expectations.

The second surprise is that this spontaneous and informal spiritual movement should take hold within a hierarchical, stylized liturgical system like Catholicism. Emotional expressions of religion had long been tamed, brought under control, or at least conventionalized, in the Catholic Church, particularly in the Irish-Anglo version that is typical of the United States. There was no room for outbursts of spiritual enthusiasm, spontaneous prayer and prophecy, handclapping and the joyful singing of hymns. This is the kind of thing one would expect to witness in a revivalist tent full of rural Holy Rollers.

There was indeed a liturgical movement that introduced new modes of worship in the Catholic Church, demanding vernacular participation by the congregation, and loosening up the staid and traditional practices of the past. It too became routinized, with the parish priest almost always using the shortest second eucharistic prayer, and the congregation using the perfunctory handshake (where it was allowed at all) for the so-called kiss of peace. The charismatic prayer meeting, with or without the Eucharist, has changed all that. Intellectual understanding of the worship service no longer seems as important as an emotional feeling of fellowship with both God and other human beings.

Another surprise of the renewal is that it has attracted large numbers of economically comfortable people of considerable formal education. The Pentecostal style of religion had previously been associated mainly with lower-class people of simple faith and little formal schooling. Who would have expected that highly educated faculty members of a university would get the first inspiration to inaugurate the charismatic renewal among American Catholics? The chronicle is clear on this: the movement got under way in 1967 at Duquesne University, and then spread out to Notre Dame University, the University of Michigan and other centers of learning.

In the survey we made of lay Catholic charismatics we found that about two-thirds of them had attended and/or finished college and that relatively few are in blue-collar occupations. This may be partly due to the fact that the initial leadership came from the college campus and the university faculty, but there appears to be no inherent reason in the ideology and practices of the movement that would discourage membership from the lower ranks of occupations. Hardly any black Catholics are involved, and some of the better educated among them tend to identify the renewal with the "shouting" religions they find among poor, rural, and Protestant blacks.

A fourth and unanticipated element in this renewal movement is that it was initiated by lay people and still remains largely under the control of the laity. In other places and at other times one may have expected that the founder of a vigorous religious revival would be a pious priest or ascetic religious who came out of the monastery to crusade for souls. What may be of even greater interest is that when these lay leaders wanted to learn the "mechanics" of charismatic spirituality they turned for counsel, not to the Catholic clergy, but to Protestant Pentecostal ministers. They continue to be wary of ecclesiastical control and have no intention of being enveloped in the clerical and canonical system of the Church.

It would be wrong to suggest that Catholic Pentecostals do not like priests or feel that they have no need of the clergy. In fact, they deplore the dearth of Spirit-filled clergy and try to convert priests to the movement. There may be some seeds of anticlericalism among them, but this is played down when lay leaders like Paul de Celles and Kevin Ranaghan get themselves ordained to the diaconate. What seems to be happening here is a new and different kind of clergy-lay relationship. There is a healthy respect for priests on the lay side, while more and more priests are developing a mature respect for the laity. The charismatics are now being taken seriously by the clergy and by an increasing number of previously cautious bishops.

As a sociologist of religion I must confess that these four characteristics of the charismatic renewal were not anticipated by the social scientists whose business it is to study such trends. The experts did not foresee that a new spiritual movement (a) would be inaugurated by lay Catholics, (b) attract adherents from the better advantaged middle class, (c) arouse a preference for the emotional over the intellectual experience of the faith, and (d) emerge in the midst of the scientific, rational American culture. If the Catholic hierarchy has been cautious about this development, the social scientists have been perplexed by it.

Traditionalist Tendencies

In a sense, what is happening here seems to be a manifestation of the "counter-culture," a reflection of what Charles Reich has called "Consciousness III." Ordinarily we associate this notion with hippie-type youth and street people who flaunt the bourgeois conformities of American society, or with the underprivileged poor in the ghetto who are alienated from the capitalistic values of the American culture. They are sociologically notable because they do not think and act "normally," that is, they differ from the behavior patterns that are widely acceptable to the majority. The Catholic Pentecostal also tends to defy the conventional Catholic patterns of religious expression.

This Catholic counter-culture movement must not be interpreted in terms of the liberal-conservative contrasts in the general society. The members argue that these words lose their meaning when a person turns to God and receives the charisms of the Holy Spirit. From the point of view of religious practices there is certainly a "liberalizing" tendency of prayerful spontaneity and almost uninhibited spiritual enthusiasm. On the other hand, there is a tendency to turn to the traditional, Bible-centered concepts and practices in human relations. One may well call this a "conservative" tendency.

There are two examples of this traditional frame of mind found widely among Catholic charismatics. The first is their attitude on the status of women, and the other is a turning away from the social action approach that has characterized much of official Church policy in recent decades. While American society is moving toward a greater emancipation of women in all areas of life, the Pentecostals are preaching a kind of biblical subordination of women. While the Church itself is promoting organized crusades for social justice, the charismatics are focusing on the individual practice of the corporal works of mercy.

The majority of lay Pentecostals are against the women's liberation movement and they are also unfavorable to the proposal of ordination of women to the priesthood. In this respect they probably reflect the attitudes of the general Catholic lay population, but the more pertinent question deals with the role and status of women within the charismatic movement itself. Approximately two-thirds of all "members," that is, people who regularly attend prayer meetings and show the greatest enthusiasm for the movement, are women. They exert an influence that is truly charismatic and also perform those necessary and mundane ministries that are usually done by women's auxiliaries to men's organizations. From this point of view they enact a "principal role" in the functioning of more than forty percent of the prayer groups.

There are well-known lay women, like Patti Gallagher and Barbara Schlemon, and some religious sisters who lecture at regional and diocesan conferences. Many women attend daytime prayer meetings which are organized and led by one of their number. In the highly structured Word of God community at Ann Arbor women fill the office of "handmaid," usually ministering to other women, but none holds a leadership office among the community coordinators. At the top level of decision-making in the national organization it is the male voice that speaks with authority. The management and editing of the movement periodical, *New Covenant*, are exclusively in male hands.

Whatever the participation of women at the lower echelons of the charismatic renewal, the ideology of the movement runs counter to the general American trend toward the greater emancipation of women. This is particularly underlined in the Pentecostal writings and teachings on family relations and the subordination of the wife to the authority of the husband. The theological analogy recommends that just as the Son is in obedience to the divine Father, so also should the wife and children be in obedience to the head of the family. This appears to be the underpinning of the general charismatic attitude toward women, and it is questioned by Pentecostal feminists in some of the less organized prayer groups. At any rate, it flies in the face of the contemporary American feminist ideology.

The second example of a traditionalist attitude among charismatics is in the area of organized social action. This has been the subject of much debate among the movement leaders and it constantly revolves around the primary purpose of the renewal. This is not a question of unfavorable social attitudes to the larger problems of American society. Our survey reveals that the majority of lay Pentecostals have sympathy for the civil rights movement, the Chicano farm workers, and the social problems of poverty, health and housing. On the other hand, less than twenty percent of them have been actively engaged in organized movements of social reform and this probably reflects a similar proportion of conventional lay Catholics not so engaged.

Charismatics come together at their prayer meetings to praise and worship God. They have experienced a personal conversion, symbolized in baptism of the Spirit and expressed in witness and prophecy and in the speaking in tongues. Members in regular attendance know each other's first names; they embrace each other joyously; they have a clear sense of fellowship of the chosen children of God. As one Pentecostal priest asked me: "Why do you want them to be something else? Why do you expect them to organize on picket lines and join civil rights demonstrations and clean up City Hall?" The blunt and pragmatic fact is that prayer groups would be torn apart if the members attempted to find agreement on which side to take in social controversy.

The goal of the charismatic movement is personal spiritual reform and not organized social reform. The basic conviction is that a better society can emerge only when there are better people. Yet it would be completely erroneous to interpret this as an individualistic and self-centered attitude. Catholic Pentecostals are deeply involved on a person-to-person basis with people who are in need. Among the New Orleans prayer groups this is an emphasized ministry, as it probably is in other places. The members are inspired to the performance of the corporal works of mercy: helping youth in trouble, paying the rent for a poor family, visiting the lonely, the elderly and the sick. At this level of social action the charismatic Catholic appears to be far in advance of the conventional Catholic.

Inevitable Routinization

After looking at the unexpected and the unconventional aspects of the Pentecostal renewal, it may be helpful to note that the natural development of the movement, while underplayed by the charismatics, could have been foreseen by the sociologist. There is no intention to deny that the renewal is the surprise of the Holy Spirit, that it is God at work among his people, that it is he who leads it and keeps it going. Having said that, we must also say that the renewal is subject to the same laws of development that characterize all growing social organizations.

Despite frequent protests by charismatic spokesmen that this is not an organization or structure, or even a movement, the original enthusiastic spontaneity has evolved into institutionalized behavior and routinized structure. There is no way that this can be avoided short of chaos, as Francis found out with his mendicant monks, and Ignatius found out with his contemplative actionists. The sheer multiplication of membership forces attention to the need for rational organization.

From the point of view of structure, the charismatic renewal has developed fairly clear-cut lines of leadership, power and authority. No single individual is the elected president or the proclaimed prophet of the whole movement; nobody wants to assume authority, but the fact is that authority is exercised throughout the movement. At the core of the organization is the Renewal Service Committee, composed of nine men who meet eight times a year. The Renewal Advisory Committee is made up of twenty-five males and two females. The annual National Service Conference attracts leaders from all over the country.

A happy slogan among charismatics is that "the only authority is the authority of service," and this is why the top management of the movement calls itself a Service Committee. One need only be a faithful reader of *New Covenant* to learn the names of the movers and shakers, the decision-makers, of the whole organization. The system of government is vaguely representative in the sense that leaders "emerge" from the membership as they display qualities of enthusiasm, competence, intelligence and discernment. If the authority structure has to have an ecclesiastical name, it is probably presbyterian rather than episcopal or congregational.

This is true also at the level of the local community of charismatics, where one finds households and core groups, leaders and coordinators.

The nomenclature has not completely jelled: what is a pastoral team in one area may be called a coordinating committee in another. Within these prayer groups there are as many ministries as there are group functions to be performed or services to be rendered. Even though inspiration is pure and motivation is inspired, these functions do not just "happen." There is obvious planning and division of labor and assignment of tasks. To be successful all of this requires organization, and one wonders why there is so much resistance to expressing this fact in ordinary sociological terminology.

A central and unsolved organizational problem still faces the whole Pentecostal renewal: this is the concept of the "covenant community." The people at Ann Arbor and South Bend, who control the press and communication channels of the movement, are making a strong pitch for a kind of rigid, highly structured and self-enclosed Christian community. J. Massingberd Ford distinguishes this from the many charismatic prayer groups that are more loosely structured, less authoritarian and more likely to be absorbed into the mainstream of Catholic life. As yet there is no formal split between these two organizational concepts and the total charismatic movement may be ultimately broad enough to embrace both.

Rick Smolan

HOW SHALL WE RELATE TO CHURCH?

Ralph Martin

Today God is calling Christians of all denominations to complete unity. Probably no spiritual renewal movement in history has cut through denominational barriers as successfully as the charismatic renewal. A brief look at the origins and evolution of this renewal in Christianity reveals its deep potential as a source of the unity to which God is calling us.

Ralph Martin edits *New Covenant* magazine and serves as a coordinator of the 900-member Word of God Community in Ann Arbor, Michigan. He has been a leader in the charismatic movement since its beginnings.

The Classical Pentecostals

The first stage of the charismatic renewal is commonly called the classical Pentecostal movement. At the turn of this century, a group of Christians gathered in a farmhouse in Topeka, Kansas in order to discover the key to vital Christianity. Together they studied the Acts of the

Apostles and were impressed by the extraordinary way in which the early Christians experienced the power of the Holy Spirit in their lives. As the early Christians preached the Good News of Jesus Christ, their words were accompanied by astounding signs: speaking in tongues, prophecy, and healings. This small group of Christians prayed that they too might experience the power of the Holy Spirit in their lives, and many of them received a tremendous outpouring of the Holy Spirit. They called this release of the Spirit in their lives the "baptism of the Holy Spirit," and it was accompanied by the same phenomena that occurred among the early Christians, such as speaking in tongues, prophecy, and healings.

Shortly thereafter, other Christians from Holiness churches and from the historic Protestant churches also began to experience the baptism of the Holy Spirit and live a dynamic Christian life. However, when they returned to their respective denominations with this good news, they were generally met with rejection. The theology of most of the churches at that time universally interpreted the charismatic gifts as something exclusively for the early Church. These people were told that what they were experiencing surely was from the devil or that they were psychologically unbalanced. As a result, the first major stage of the charismatic renewal developed its own denominational structure as people were forced to leave their original churches. Until now, their contact with the historical churches has been almost nil because of the rejection they suffered at the beginning of the century.

Today there are numerous Pentecostal denominations, and most of them experience a remarkably vital Christianity. An estimated 13,000,000 people belong to these Pentecostal denominations. Their impact is being felt throughout the world, and in some places their growth rate is ten times greater than any other Christian church. For example, almost 1/3 of the Christians in Chile belong to Pentecostal churches. The largest church in the world is presently being built by a Pentecostal denomination in Brazil. It will seat 25,000 people upon completion.

The Neo-Pentecostal Movement

The second big wave in the charismatic renewal took place between the years 1957-1967 and is often called the neo-Pentecostal movement. Once again Protestants in the mainline, historical denominations began to receive the baptism in the Holy Spirit and experience the gifts of the Spirit such as speaking in tongues, prophecy, and healing. This time they were, generally speaking, not forced to leave their churches.

The public appearance of this stage in the charismatic renewal is probably the result of widespread national and international publicity given to the case of Rev. Dennis Bennett. Fr. Bennett, an Episcopalian clergyman, was baptized in the Holy Spirit and told his congregation in California about his experience. As a result, he was forced to leave his church in California, but the Episcopalian bishop of the state of Washington was sympathetic to his plight and offered him a position in a parish in Seattle. Today he is the rector of a flourishing charismatic parish there, St. Luke's Church.

It wasn't easy in the early days of the neo-Pentecostal movement to experience the baptism of the Holy Spirit and stay within your church. In fact, if you were a Presbyterian minister in those days in some parts of this country and admitted being baptized in the Spirit, it is very likely that your synod was doing everything in its power to get you out of the church. Eventually, most of the major Protestant denominations came to grips with what was happening in their midst. The American Baptist Convention, one of the Lutheran synods, and some of the Presbyterian bodies issued cautious and by no means enthusiastic statements on the Pentecostal experience. These statements didn't approve the Pentecostal experience, but neither did they completely reject those who claimed to have had the experience.

This wave in the charismatic renewal took over many of the characteristics of the classical Pentecostal movement. Although they generally weren't forced to leave their churches, many Protestants who were baptized in the Holy Spirit at this time took a critical attitude toward the church and developed anti-institutional tendencies. Often they ended up staying within their church more out of security or strategy than out of a deep faith that God would renew the institional church to which they belonged. They often took on a biblical fundamentalism that relied too heavily on exegetical weaknesses found in classical Pentecostal theology. In many cases people in this wave of the renewal would adopt what Fr. Kilian McDonnell, a leading Catholic expert on Pentecostalism, calls "cultural baggage"—the ways of speaking, phraseology, and styles of prayer and worship that came from classical Pentecostalism but were not necessarily the best way of communicating with mainline Protestants.

It is difficult to say how many people are active in the neo-Pentecostal movement because it's totally unstructured and doesn't constitute a separate denomination. In addition, Protestants in this movement often meet through the vehicle of interdenominational conferences and organizations such as the Full Gospel Businessmen's Association. It is estimated that approximately 10% of the Episcopalian clergy is active in the neo-Pentecostal renewal. Conservatively speaking, there are hundreds of thousands of people from the historic Protestant churches who are involved.

The Catholic Charismatic Renewal

The third stage of the charismatic renewal is the Catholic charismatic renewal. In 1967 a group of faculty and students at Duquesne University in Pittsburgh, a Catholic university run by the Holy Ghost Fathers, came into contact with some literature from the Pentecostal movement and began to attend a small prayer meeting held by a group of people who were part of the neo-Pentecostal movement. Their contact with the Pentecostal movement was the climax of a long search they had begun for the key to a more vital and powerful Christianity. Soon they themselves as a group experienced the baptism of the Holy Spirit and began to tell other Catholics about their experience. Because a number of these people were theologians and Catholics out of conviction rather than culture, they were in a very good position to articulate the meaning of the Pentecostal experience in terms that a Catholic can understand.

The charismatic renewal has developed very rapidly in the Catholic Church. Shortly after its appearance, an international conference was held at the University of Notre Dame for those who were active in the nascent movement. Slightly over 100 people attended. It was international by virtue of the presence of one nun from Canada. Last June, at the Eighth International Conference on the Charismatic Renewal in the Catholic Church, 30,000 people were present, including groups from 40 different countries.

A little over three years ago, a group of people started publishing a monthly magazine for the charismatic renewal called *New Covenant*. It began with a circulation of 1,000. Today its circulation is approaching 50,000. Several years ago, the Communication Center for the Catholic charismatic renewal at Notre Dame began to print a directory of Catholic charismatic prayer groups. Three years ago, there were 600 groups listed. Last year there were 1,200 groups listed. This year there are almost 2,400 groups listed in over 54 different countries.

The charismatic renewal in the Catholic Church isn't limited to the United States. It has experienced a remarkable expansion throughout the world. This year over Pentecost weekend, Catholic charismatics in Australia held their first national conference in Melbourne. Almost 2,000 of Australia's estimated 7,000 Catholic charismatics attended the closing session of the conference in St. Patrick's Cathedral. In New Zealand, over 3,000 Catholics are active in the charismatic renewal, which is a very high number in proportion to the Catholic population of that country. In June, the first French language conference on the charismatic renewal was held in Quebec City, Canada, and 10,000 people were there.

The charismatic renewal in Latin America has also developed rapidly. Last year a conference was held in Bototá, Colombia for leaders in the Catholic charismatic renewal in Latin America. A little over 30 leaders attended. This year, another conference was held and over 200 leaders were present. A communication center has been set up in Puerto Rico for the Latin American charismatic renewal which publishes a sister publication to *New Covenant* in Spanish called *Alabare.* It has been in existence for a little over a year and is already being received by 3,000 people in Latin America. The charismatic renewal is only two years old in France, but there are already 10,000 French Catholics active and leaders predict that the number will probably double and maybe even quadruple in the coming year. Since the Catholic charismatic renewal is growing so rapidly, it is difficult to estimate the number of Catholics involved. A conservative estimate, based on literature published and surveys sent to prayer groups would be 350,000 worldwide as of this writing.

Unlike the first two stages of the charismatic renewal during this century, the Catholic charismatic renewal has received a sympathetic response from the hierarchy of the Church. Over the past year almost every American cardinal has made a positive pastoral response to the charismatic renewal. Cardinal Madeiros of Boston and Cardinal Manning of Los Angeles have written letters to the priests in their dioceses encouraging them to come into personal contact with the charismatic renewal and to give it a positive response at the parish level. Last Pentecost, Cardinal Dearden of Detroit celebrated a charismatic liturgy in the cathedral to which all Catholic charismatics in the archdiocese were invited. For the first time in years the cathedral was filled as 2,000 people crowded inside. On the same day, Cardinal Krol of Philadelphia invited the Catholic charismatic prayer groups in his diocese to attend a Pentecostal celebration, and 2,000 came. Cardinal Carberry of St. Louis has set up a regular monthly meeting with leaders of the charismatic renewal in his diocese with whom he meets personally.

On the international level, Cardinal Arns of Sao Paulo, Brazil is positively supporting the charismatic renewal and last year invited David du Plessis, an elder statesman in the classical Pentecostal movement, to speak to numerous groups in his diocese. Bishop Alfonso Uribe Jaramillo of Sonson-Rionegro, Colombia is associated with the charismatic renewal and is now one of the leading spokesman for the renewal in Latin America.

An increasing number of bishops have themselves experienced a deep spiritual renewal in the charismatic renewal and are now personally involved. There are perhaps 15 bishops around the world who have been baptized in the Holy Spirit and have experienced the gifts of the Spirit. Bishop Joseph McKinney of Grand Rapids, Michigan was one of the first bishops to be baptized in the Holy Spirit and is now serving as liaison between the Catholic charismatic renewal and the Roman Catholic hierarchy. The most prominent member of the hierarchy to make a major commitment to what God is doing in the charismatic renewal thus far is Cardinal Leon Josef Suenens of Malines-Brussels, Belgium.

Last October, a group of 120 leaders in the charismatic renewal from all over the world met in Rome, Italy for a small conference to discuss the international development of the charismatic renewal. At that time, Pope Paul VI received a small group of these leaders in a special audience and encouraged their efforts of spiritual renewal. He said, "We rejoice with you, dear friends, at the renewal of spiritual life manifested in the Church today, in different forms and in different environments. Certain common notes appear in this renewal: the taste for deep prayer, personal and in groups, a return to contemplation and an emphasizing of praise of God, the desire to devote oneself completely to Christ, a great availability for the calls of the Holy Spirit, more assiduous reading of the Scriptures, generous brotherly devotion, the will to make a contribution to the service of the Church. In all that, we can recognize the mysterious and discreet work of the Spirit, who is the soul of the Church." The charismatic renewal in the Catholic Church has developed rapidly indeed, and has gained acceptance at the highest levels of the Church.

Ecumenical Relationships in the Charismatic Renewal

The classical Pentecostal movement, the neo-Pentecostal movement and the Catholic charismatic renewal are like three rivers of God's power that are flowing in Christianity. These rivers are flowing for the most part in their own courses. But I feel that something is beginning to happen that will change these courses. I think that God is moving to make them flow together like a mighty river and out of their unity bring something to all the Christian churches. Already the charismatic renewal is extraordinarily effective ecumenically. It is breaking down barriers that exist among Christians, and where there was once prejudice, there is now a new openness. Most Catholic prayer groups are ecumenical and people of all three streams in the charismatic renewal actively participate in each other's conferences and meetings. The Holy Spirit is doing a remarkable thing through the charismatic renewal by opening Christians of different backgrounds to one another and giving them the desire to see a full and complete Christianity.

In the different elements of the charismatic renewal, we are learning things from one another. God is speaking to us through our brothers and sisters from different churches. In the Catholic charismatic renewal, God has brought us into a new realm of freedom as a result of our contact with our brothers and sisters in the classical Pentecostal and neo-Pentecostal movements. We are learning that as we preach the Gospel with confidence and boldness, Jesus wants to reach out and confirm our words with amazing signs that will attest to his power and presence in the world today.

An ecumenical shockwave has hit the classical Pentecostals. For a long time, after being rejected by the institutional churches, they had in turn rejected the institutional churches. In the world view of Christianity that most classical Pentecostals shared, the major Protestant churches barely qualified as Christian and the Catholic Church was looked upon as fulfilling the dire predictions of the anti-Christ and whore of Babylon found in the book of Revelation. It has been a traumatic experience for them to see large segments of the Catholic Church and even high Catholic Church officials embracing the reality of the baptism of the Holy Spirit, including the charismatic gifts, and boldly proclaiming Jesus Christ as Lord and Savior. Consequently, they have had to reconsider their vision of what God is doing in the world and in Christianity.

Now classical Pentecostals are showing signs of openness and are even significantly involved with their fellow Christians around the world. One Brazilian Pentecostal group has joined the World Council of Churches. This is an extraordinary development because until now most Pentecostal groups have refused to have any type of contact with the historic Protestant Churches.

At the same time, many neo-Pentecostals are reconsidering what their relationship to their churches should really be. They have seen the successful integration of the charismatic renewal into the Catholic Church. As a result, they now view the baptism of the Holy Spirit not as an individual experience but as something that God wants to affect their whole church. During the past few years, groups similar to the Catholic Charismatic Renewal Service Committee, which has been instrumental in helping the charismatic renewal become related to the broader Catholic Church and not a separatist group, have formed in major Protestant denominations. In 1973 the Episcopalian Charismatic Fellowship and the Lutheran Coordinating Committee were established. Groups that already existed, such as the Charismatic Communion of Presbyterian Ministers that was formed in 1966 and the American Baptist Charismatic Fellowship founded in 1968, began to get a new vision of what God wants to do through the charismatic renewal. They no longer considered themselves mutual protection societies where they could escape the criticism of their fellow ministers, but as instruments of a positive renewal in the Christian churches.

In these three rivers of the charismatic renewal that are flowing among the people of God, I see a major and incalculable power for Christian unity. In the past few months, I think there have been some remarkable changes in the course of these three rivers that will make them an even more effective witness of Christian unity to wider churches. Even though these rivers initially sprang forth in America, each one of them has become an international force so that all three elements in the charismatic renewal are now mighty rivers flowing throughout Christianity worldwide. I think that they will be not only a remarkable contribution to Christian unity, but a source of international unity.

In the Catholic charismatic renewal,

I feel that we've gone on from the apologetic stage in which we laid the groundwork of properly relating to our own Church, and now, building on that, we have entered a more prophetic stage in which we can really speak out and work for the radical changes that need to happen in all the Christian churches if we are to become one, effective, visible body of Christ in the world today.

Can You Institutionalize The Spirit?

John Glaser

Donald L. Gelpi

An overworked university professor assumes extra duty with a heavy heart. It was, then, with a certain wistfulness that I cradled my phone not long ago. Against all my tired instincts, I had just agreed to help a student in another university to prepare an oral defense of a theology of the gifts of the Holy Spirit.

Donald Gelpi, S.J. is professor of theology at the Jesuit School of Theology in Berkeley. He has written two books on the charismatic movement: *Pentecostalism* and *Pentecostal Piety* (Paulist Press).

The student was involved in a charismatic prayer group and was interested in deepening her understanding of the theology of charismatic prayer. A graduate student in a Catholic institution, she had been unable to find a single member of the faculty who felt inclined to direct such a project. She had turned to me as a last resort.

I recount the incident because it seems to epitomize some of the deeper issues implied in the question to which I have been asked to speak in this article: "If you have the Gospel and the gifts of the Spirit, why do you need the institutional Church?"

Interestingly enough a similar question was put to the student in the course of her oral defense. And her answer was perceptive and right to the point. "The gifts are given," she replied, "for the renewal and upbuilding of the institutional Church. You can't respond to the gifts without dedicating yourself to the renewal of the institutional Church."

The Gospel is preached for the same purpose: to build up a community of shared faith and love, whose collective growth in the life of the Spirit is mediated by institutional structures that seek to give authentic expression to the charismatic impulses of the Spirit.

The incident retained for me a certain symbolic meaning. To begin with, the student's original dilemma is not atypical of the problem facing too many charismatic Catholics. When they turn to professional teachers in the institutional Church for theological enlightenment concerning the gifts of the Spirit and their place in Roman Catholic piety, they are apt to be greeted either with blank stares or with a scrambling attempt to toss the charismatic hot potato to someone else.

Second, the question was raised in the seminar by someone who was not actually involved in a charismatic prayer group. For the charismatic student herself, the question was a non-question, based on a shallow understanding of the meaning of Gospel, gifts, and Church.

Nor was the student's response atypical of charismatic Catholics in general. At the International Conference for the Catholic Charismatic Renewal held last summer at Notre Dame, almost every reference to loyalty to hierarchical, institutional Catholicism brought the crowd of 22,000 people to a standing ovation. And recent sociological studies of charismatic Catholics confirm the judgment that they are as a group deeply loyal to the hierarchical, institutional Church. Indeed, their enthusiasm for institutional religion often leaves the liberal Roman Catholic of the disillusioned 1960's somewhat bewildered.

There are, then, serious indications that the unhealthy opposition of charism and institution is much more of a problem for Catholics who do not frequent charismatic prayer groups than for those who do.

Third, the reasons offered by the student for rejecting such an opposition were not only theologically sound, but they were realistic in their assessment of the problems and inauthenticities which plague many of the present institutionalized expressions of Catholic piety.

But not everything is completely rosy in charismatic circles. Along with genuine protestations of institutional loyalty, one also discovers symptoms of potential divisiveness. The movement from its earliest stages has developed in part under the influence of Protestant Pentecostalism. In more than one instance, Catholic charismatics have tended to absorb the "cultural baggage" of the Protestant tradition along with some of its authentic religious insights. Among the authentic insights of Protestant Pentecostalism is its insistence on the importance and availability of the gifts of the Spirit. But its cultural baggage sometimes includes a simplistic biblical fundamentalism, an unhealthy otherworldliness, a lack of active social and political involvement, and an untenable theological theory of religious conversion.

There is pastoral and statistical evidence which indicates that the most serious problems among Catholic charismatics are the result of premature ecumenical contacts between fundamentalistic Protestant Pentecostals and relatively uneducated Catholic charismatics. These problems are, moreover, compounded when they are greeted by indifference or hostility on the part of the official Church and its teachers.

A classical Protestant Pentecostal theory of conversion separates the experience of conversion from the reception of the Holy Spirit. It designates the latter as a "second blessing" over and above conversion. And it regards tongues as the only decisive sign of the reception of the Spirit.

There is no way to reconcile such a theory with Catholic doctrine, although Catholic sacramental theology does look upon confirmation as a "second sending" of the Holy Spirit over and above the grace of baptism. Moreover, even though there is no evidence that Catholic charismatics as a group subscribe in principle to a Protestant Pentecostal theology of the "second blessing," still many of them have absorbed some of the rhetoric and religious attitudes which are the cultural concomitants of a classical Pentecostal theory of conversion. Some speak, for example, of "*the* baptism in the Holy Spirit" as though transformation in the Spirit were not a lifetime process. Or they refer to tongues as "the fullness of the Spirit." Such misleading rhetoric needs to be countered by sound teaching. But in too many instances the needed teachers fail to materialize. The negative consequences of their absence is, moreover, compounded when the official Church assumes a Gamaliel-like, wait-and-see attitude.

The Catholic charismatic renewal is, then, suffering from a vacuum in its pastoral catechesis. The national leadership has made serious efforts to fill that vacuum, but the movement has grown to the point where no national committee will be able to meet its pastoral needs. There are not enough teachers around who can relate a gift-centered, Spirit-centered piety to traditional forms of Catholic, eucharistic, sacramental worship. There is, however, solid basis in the official pastoral catechesis for effecting the needed integration of charismatic and Catholic piety.

It is no exaggeration that the bulk of nineteenth-century Catholic ecclesiology and sacramentology developed with scarcely a glance at the gifts of the Spirit. With the advent of the twentieth century, a gradual shift began to develop in the official pastoral catechesis. The encyclical *Divinum illud munus*, issued by Leo XIII in 1881, called attention to the deplorable ignorance of most Catholics concerning the Spirit and his role in the salvific process. *Mystici corporis,* issued by Pius XII, seemed to vindicate a permanent place for a charismatic element within institutional Christianity.

Prior to the Second Vatican Council, Rahner and Congar laid the initial groundwork for the quantum leap in official pastoral teaching concerning the gifts which emerged in the documents of Vatican II. Interestingly enough, however, in the early debates of the Second Vatican Council, neither the gifts nor the Holy Spirit formed a major focus of concern. The entire schema on the liturgy was passed without a mention of either—a fact which raises interesting questions about the theological gaps in the liturgical and sacramental theology which produced the liturgical reforms passed by the Council. The omission suggests that the theological speculation which had produced the liturgical renewal had developed in the kind of obtuseness to the role of the Spirit and his gifts which has too often characterized Catholic continental theology.

Debate about the Holy Spirit and about the place of the gifts in Catholic piety did not emerge within the Council until the debates turned to the schema on the Church. The initial confrontation took place between Cardinal Ruffini and and Cardinal Suenens. Cardinal Ruffini criticized the revised schema on the Church for not emphasizing enough the hierarchical, institutional character of the Church. Cardinal Suenens replied that, on the contrary, the schema failed to emphasize enough the charismatic function of the laity in the Church. Suenens was soon seconded by the Oriental-rite bishops, and eventually their combined voices carried the day.

The conceptual association of "charismatic" with "laity" and of "hierarchy" with "Church" was not untypical of the mind-set of Roman Catholics in general as they began the experience of Vatican II. But the dangers latent in too rigid and exclusive an association of these terms is obvious. For it would suggest that the laity are not really the Church and that the hierarchy cannot be charismatic. The charismatic theology which eventually emerged from Vatican II made it clear, however, that poth positions are untenable.

The Council documents make no bones about the fact that the Spirit's activity renders God in some real sense visibly present in the world. The Spirit-filled community is at one point described as a "quasi-incarnation" of the third person of the Trinity. The Church is not, of course, a repetition of the hypostatic union.

Transformation in the Spirit does not obliterate the human person. It leads persons to salvific fulfillment. But the *Dogmatic Constitution on the Church* does make the following suggestive observation: "Just as the assumed nature inseparably united to the divine Word serves him as a living instrument of salvation, so in a similar way does the communal structure of the Church serve Christ's Spirit, who vivifies it by way of building up the body" (*Lumen gentium*, n.7).

Among the ecclesial structures which the Council singles out as products of the Spirit's vivifying activity are: Sacred Scripture, the sacraments, the missionary activity of the Church, and the apostolates of the laity and of the hierarchy.

The document on revelation affirms that the Word of Scripture, when illumined by the anointing of the Spirit, is transformed into a "living and efficient word" which actually transforms in turn the lives and hearts of believers. It was, indeed, for this purpose that the biblical writings were originally inspired: namely to "impart the Word of God himself without change, and make the voice of the Holy Spirit resound in the words of the prophets and apostles" (*Nostra aetate*, nn. 11, 21).

The sacramental words of the Church also derive their power and efficacy from the anointing of the Holy Spirit. Through the sacraments (and especially through the eucharist) the Spirit inspires charity and its works in the hearts of believers (*Apostolicam actuositatem*, n.3).

The Council documents insist on the charismatic character of the missionary vocation: "The Holy Spirit uses manifold means to arouse the missionary spirit in the Church of God, and often anticipates the action of those whose task it is to rule the life of the Church" (*Ad gentes*, n. 29).

Religious orders are described as "spiritual families" united by the power of the Spirit of Jesus, and their renewal must proceed under the guidance of the gift-giving Spirit (*Perfectae caritatis*, n. 2).

Moreover, in addition to the natural human rights and duties common to all men, the charisms of the Spirit are presented as grounding the spiritual rights and duties of the faithful within the institutional Church. Whoever is called by God to serve the institutional Church through the reception of a charism has the right and duty to exercise his gift as long as he does so for the upbuilding of the community (*Apostolicam actuositatem*, n. 3).

In the Council documents the apostolate of the hierarchy is also described as having a charismatic basis. The documents of Vatican II distinguish between "hierarchical" and "charismatic" gifts. The terminology is not altogether happy. It is redundant to speak of a "charismatic charism." And the distinction between "hierarchical" and "charismatic" could suggest to some that ordained Church leaders cannot by definition be charismatic people. Actually the intent of the distinction is to affirm the essentially charismatic character of true Church leadership.

The Council documents note that the apostles enjoyed outstanding spiritual gifts, and they cite the bishops as in some sense the successors to the apostles not only in responsibility but also in their charismatic endowments (*Lumen gentium*, nn. 12, 17; *Apostolicam actuositatem*, n. 17).

It is the duty and official right of Church leaders to discern the source of the different charismatic impulses which emerge in the community. They also have the responsibility, however, to judge those impulses correctly and not to stand in the way of or suppress any legitimate charismatic impulse of the Spirit which emerges in the community (*Apostolicam actuositatem*, n. 3; *Ad gentes*, n. 4).

In other words, one important sign of a Spirit-filled member of the hierarchy will be his openness in expectant faith to every authentic movement of the Spirit in the community. And one important sign of a truly Christian community will be its openness in expectant faith to the pastoral direction of its ordained leaders. Only through such mutual openness can any gift be authentically discerned and used for the building up of the Church universal. For by the hierarchical gifts, the Council means those charisms which are necessary for the authentic exercise of official pastoral leadership in the Church. The most prominent hierarchical gifts are the gifts of teaching and discernment. And the latter gift is portrayed in Vatican II as the key to sound Church government.

Finally in Vatican II, the Holy Spirit is presented as a dynamic bond uniting believers everywhere. But interestingly enough, the Council documents are careful not to restrict the activity of the Spirit to the hearts of believers only. The *Pastoral Constitution on the Church in the Modern World* speaks of the Spirit of Jesus as the one who "directs the unfolding of time and renews the face of the earth." The same document affirms that the Spirit is "not absent" even from secular movements which seek humane and socially constructive ends (*Unitatis redintegratio*, n. 2; *Lumen gentium*, n. 11; *Gaudium et spes*, n. 26).

The attempt to oppose the gifts of the Spirit to institutional religion is traceable to two distinct sources in the Christian tradition.

"Inner light" Protestant pietism is a form of popular piety which has tended to emerge from disenchantment with institutional religion. The attitudes of inner light piety are present in many of the popular expressions of Protestant Pentecostalism. In places where those attitudes are absorbed uncritically by Catholic charismatics, anti-institutional attitudes can, of course, begin to infect the Catholic charismatic renewal. But such is not the present overall thrust of Catholic charismatic piety; and where Catholic charismatics are given the pastoral guidance and instruction which they have the strict right to expect from their official teachers and leaders, the evidence is that charismatic piety reinforces rather than undermines institutional loyalty.

But institutional religion has produced its own divisive version of the "inner light," when spiritual and bureaucratic rigidity prevents it from absorbing and directing legitimate charismatic impulses which emerge in its midst. "Divisive enthusiasm" has its counterpart, therefore, in "divisive institutionalism." If American Protestant Pentecostals show tendencies at times to the former, American Roman Catholics not infrequenly manifest tendencies to the latter.

The Catholic charismatic renewal gives evidence, then, of being a truly prophetic movement, for it is forcing the entire Christian community, Catholic as well as Protestant, to reexamine its attitudes to Jesus, the Spirit and the institutional Church.

It would, however, take either a blind man or a fool not to see that neither the institutional American Church nor the Catholic charismatic renewal is completely acceptable in its present form. Both are in process of creative evolution. Institutional Catholicism gives evidence, moreover, of still badly needing the kind of spiritual renewal that the charismatic renewal offers it. The charismatic renewal for its part is in need of all the gifts of the Spirit operative in the larger Christian community if it is to develop with balance and true openness to God. But one may hope that as "charismatic Catholics" and "institutional Catholics" share actively the gifts of the Spirit they have both received, the result will be what charismatic Christians throughout the world now long for: the charismatic renewal of the universal, institutional Church.

It will, perhaps, be useful to summarize in conclusion some basic points:

1. There is solid evidence that the tendency to oppose charism and institution is at present more of a problem for Catholics who are not involved in charismatic prayer groups than for those who are.

2. One reason for this tendency is inadequate catechesis which most Catholics received concerning the place of the Spirit and of his gifts in authentic Catholic piety.

3. This imbalance in Catholic catechesis has been somewhat corrected by the teachings of the popes and of Vatican II, but it has yet to be communicated effectively to a large number of Roman Catholics.

4. From a theological standpoint some reasons why the gifts of the Spirit and the message of the Gospel can never be legitimately opposed to the institutions of the Church are:

a. The Gospel has as its purpose to open the hearts of men to the charismatic anointing of the Spirit; but the gifts of the Spirit have as their purpose to shape the shared life of Christians, including those aspects of Christian life which need institutional mediation.

b. The institutional Church cannot function as an authentic quasi-sacramental revelation of God unless it comes into being as a response to the graces and gifts of the Spirit.

c. The gifts of the Spirit cannot be authentically discerned in any community which is closed in principle to the Church universal or to the voice of the Spirit as it comes to expression in all the gifts he gives, including the gifts he bestows on the hierarchy.

5. The chief historical sources for the inauthentic and misleading opposition of the charisms and the institutional Church are the misleading presuppositions of "inner light" piety and of "divisive institutionalism."

When The Cloud Of Glory Dissipates

Edward D. O'Connor

Asbury Park Press

In 1970, when most of the national magazines and papers carried articles reviewing events of the sixties, and forecasting the trends of the seventies, the charismatic renewal was scarcely mentioned.

The few people who heard of it usually reacted with incredulous smiles or stupefaction. Today this is no longer the case. The Pentecostal movement is a frequent topic of inquiry by journalists as well as scholars. Several European newspapers, and even television stations, have sent representatives to this country to prepare reports on it. In the Church itself, a clear sign of recognition is the fact that bishops are beginning to issue statements, not merely praising the movement, or cautioning people about it, but giving practical regulations for it.

Edward O'Connor, C.S.C. teaches at Notre Dame University and has worked in the Catholic Pentecostal movement since it was a spark.

This public acceptance of the renewal as a fact to be reckoned with seems to be paralleled by a development taking place within the movement itself. The freshness of new venture is being replaced by a familiar, worn look and established patterns. By now, most of those actually taking part in it have probably had two or three years of experience. They no longer gather together in a spirit of wondering anticipation; they know fairly well what to expect. Newcomers are prepared for the "baptism in the Spirit" by standardized "Life in the Spirit" seminars. There are well-defined concepts and fixed forms of such ministries as prophecy, healing, and deliverance, which would have seemed quite esoteric just a few years ago.

On another plane, there are indications of a growing concern about or disenchantment with the renewal. Some of this is occasioned precisely by the progressive organization and standardization. Some comes from mistakes that have been made or people who have been hurt. The number of those who, after taking part in charismatic prayer groups, have quit them is increasing, as likewise the number of groups that lasted a short while and then failed. Even those who are still active participants often seem to be more reserved than formerly in their commitment to the renewal, or in their expectations of it.

Such developments suggest that the movement is entering into a new phase of its existence, which I think it is important to try to understand. One approach would be to say that it has lost its first enthusiasm and is now facing the test of whether it is to have an enduring effect or to evaporate like many revivals of the past. There is a general truth in this view, which focuses attention on one of the serious problems of the renewal at the present time. There are people who, in an initial burst of generosity, accepted heavy responsibilities of leadership, witnessing, counseling and the like, but now are finding these burdensome and are beginning to drag their feet. This is an inevitable problem in a venture which depends on generosity and self-sacrifice; but it does not seem to pose any imminent peril to the continuation of the charismatic renewal, which has already established a base wide enough, and organs firm enough, to ensure its perpetuation for a long time to come, even if in a more institutionalized form.

Such an appraisal, however, for all its truth, does not take into consideration the peculiar nature of the charismatic renewal, the distinctive trait of which is to engender enthusiastic Christians. For an enthusiastic movement to lose its enthusiasm would seem tantamount to death. When an inspirational activity is perpetuated by an institution, is this perpetuation or not rather strangulation? There are certain historians who claim that this is what happened to the primitive Church. Many see the same sequence repeated in the history of later movements of renewal, revival and reform, such as Lutheranism, Methodism, the Holiness movement, and already even in some of the modern Pentecostal denominations. It would be small comfort to charismatics to be assured that they are simply drifting into the same inexorable pattern. This explains why there is a chronic, although in the long run ineffectual, tendency among charismatics to resist all organization and institution as a quenching of the Spirit.

It is even more important to recognize that the enthusiasm of charismatics does not come from an idea by which they have been persuaded, but from experience of a reality, as they at any rate believe. They have touched the fingers of God and have felt the renewing power of his love. Prayer groups and covenant communities have sprung up, not on the basis of some religious doctrine or socio-political theory, but because the love of God poured forth in hearts by the Holy Spirit has opened up possibilities of human communion which they would never have dreamed of.

Charismatics are not all sentimental optimists trying to project reality onto empty words by an over-excited imagination. Many of them are hard-headed, practical "realists" who have simply been stopped in their tracks by encounter with a Reality against which their own devices have smashed. Their personal experience, interpreted in the light of Christ's promises and St. Paul's doctrine, convinced them that the Holy Spirit himself is the source of the energy and vitality of the charismatic renewal. Hence they expect it to have an impact not commensurable with those of more human programs of reform.

To tell such people that their movement is going the way of all others is to question its fundamental validity. It would mean either that the whole experience was an illusion, or that if the Spirit ever had any part in it, contact with him is already being lost. In fact, it seems to be precisely this inference that is leading some people to abandon the charismatic renewal and others, who remain in it, to strive mightily to recover its initial fervor.

Without denying that part of the present experience can indeed be explained in terms of simple attrition and spent enthusiasm, I would like to propose two other considerations which I believe will shed light on the deeper meaning of what is taking place. The first is that experience of the charismatic operation of the Spirit is prone to arouse undue expectations. People sense that the kingdom of God is somehow being realized among them, and the re-emergence of petty human frailties which they thought has been transcended may come as a crushing disillusionment. To dismiss this as the inevitable fate of the optimism that gathers around any new movement is to misconstrue its distinctive motivation. Charismatics are those who have "experienced the power of the age to come," inherent in which is the sure promise of the realization of a heavenly Jerusalem that is already in the making. The Holy Spirit is power of the risen Lord at work in the world, the very power that is to bring about the fullness of the kingdom. To know him is to be in living contact with the kingdom in its coming. This is why St. Paul insisted that the gift of the Spirit is the pledge or earnest money of the good things we await.

Where the early Christians looked for the parousia to come in their lifetime, Pentecostals are often tempted to expect an immediate and perfect sanctification. In both cases, the error is due not so much to a misunderstanding of Jesus' words as to an over-eagerness aroused by the Spirit's power to fulfill God's promises completely. The disciples of the first century had to be reassured that "with the Lord, one day is like a thousand years, and a thousand years like one day." Pentecostals are perhaps more in need of the lesson that runs throughout the letter to the Hebrews: that it is not enough to "have tasted the heavenly gift, and become partakers of the Holy Spirit"; we need also to "hold our first confidence firm to the end."

The true picture of our situation is given by St. Paul: we have only "the first fruits of the Spirit"; consequently, we must "groan inwardly" as we wait for our redemption to be completed. The work of the Spirit in us is genuine, but not yet complete, and the very touch of its reality intensifies our agony at what it lacks. The image of God has really been imprinted on us, but our "carnal nature," not yet fully subdued, will continue for a long time to reassert itself and disfigure that image. All this must be taken into consideration if we are not to make excessive demands on ourselves and others.

A second consideration is that in the dynamics of grace, there is a regime of beginnings that is not meant to be perpetuated indefinitely, but to be followed by a different regime more suitable for deepening and strengthening the life of the Spirit. This happens quite normally in the lives of individuals, and there is no reason to doubt that it happens likewise to communities, and even to an entire movement. Thus the beginning of life in the Spirit often seems more blessed than its sequel. This applies particularly to that new beginning, or second conversion, by which an adult turns to God consciously and deliberately, with a personal conviction that had not been present in his juvenile religious life. Such a conversion is not rarely brought about by an overwhelming grace that fills the person with a vivid awareness of the reality of God's presence and love. Under the influence of this grace one experiences new unity in his being, a new life and goodness in the world around him, and a new harmony in relating to it. If this grace endures for a time, the person may have the impression that all his faults and difficulties have been vanquished by the gentle and sweet dominion of a Lord whose sovereignty embraces all in perfect concord.

But this sort of grace never endures for long, and as it slips gradually away, like an ebbing sea, the harsh, ugly and banal things it had covered begin to reappear. No matter how desperately a man may try, he can do nothing to retain this grace, nor achieve anything that duplicates it. It is a purely gratuitous gift that is bestowed for a moment and withdrawn when its time is over. Meanwhile it has served the useful purpose of shaking us up, dissolving our previous patterns and outlook, giving us a new vision, reorienting our lives, getting us off the pad, and starting us on a new course, like St. Paul at Damascus. God has invaded the little world of our construction and let us know that in being possessed by him, as in no other way, we have life, healing, deliverance, and restoration.

But before this can be fully and definitively realized, we are required to respond to grace by a personal effort of our own. The spontaneous and loving assent elicited under the impact of God's presence must be ratified by faithful endurance of trial and offering of sacrifice. The crucified Lord is not content with disciples who quit him at the first hard saying; he seeks those to whom he can say, "You are those who have persevered with me in my affliction."

He therefore withdraws this initial grace, not of course cutting us off completely (in which case we would utterly collapse), but sustaining us by a more hidden power that does not have such manifest fruits of peace and harmony. Then our weaknesses reappear, and the faults which seemed to have been healed become operative again. One is tempted to think he has failed and lost the grace of God forever, or that it was nothing but illusion in the first place. This is a point at which many people, overwhelmed by discouragement, renounce the spiritual life at the very moment when serious progress could have begun for them.

Prayer groups and covenant communities seem to go through a similar process, although in a less sharply characterized way, since they are composed of various people at different stages of growth. In the early period of their formation, they often experience a kind of bloom time of grace. They are blessed with a spirit of loving unity in which the members find it a joy to be with one another and reach agreements with relative ease. There is a generosity in mutual service and a sincere readiness to lay down one's life for one's brother. Mistakes are readily overcome, inconveniences cheerfully borne. A lively sense of the presence of God pervades the prayer meetings. Often this is a time in which the charisms of tongues, prophecy and interpretation are just beginning to function freely, and the fresh wonder of them brings a touch of glory into the meetings. Healings and remarkable answers to prayer fill the group with awe.

Eventually, however, this "cloud of glory" dissipates. The charm wears off the charisms, and people learn to be more discriminating in both exercising and believing them. Instead of being carried forward simply by the movement of the Spirit, the activities of the community are planned and prepared. Some people become vaguely troubled by the feeling that they are simply continuing to go through the same old motions without making progress; others, especially among the leaders, grow perplexed about the direction in which they should orient their efforts. Amid this growing humanness, faults reappear and disagreements and personal rivalries spring up, leading sometimes to painful divisions.

When this happens, there is a natural temptation to look back nostalgically upon the times that have passed and to try by every way possible to recapture them. In a certain measure this is right, for we always need to beware of apathy and the recrudescence of deep-seated faults. However, it is no more possible to recover the grace of beginnings than to hold onto the golden days of childhood. The law of growth applies as inexorably to communities as to individuals. When the clapping of hands and the shouting of Hallelujah become an effort to stir up an exuberance that is no longer there, it has a terrible hollowness, like the cosmetics by which an aging woman tries to cling to the appearances of her vanishing youth.

In any case, the passing of early fervor is not grounds for discouragement, but a summons to grow in maturity. Even when it results largely from human faults, it is used by providence to teach us things which had to be learned in any case. The human planning and organization that become more prominent as a prayer community develops are not necessarily a sign of a loss of reliance on the inspiration of the Spirit; they are the human response and cooperation which God requires of those who receive his grace. They are a pledge of earnestness, an exercise that brings firmness to our faith commitment.

When the people of Israel were wandering through the desert, God nourished them with manna from heaven and guided them by a pillar of fire and smoke. After they arrived at the promised land, they had to dig their own fields and choose their own paths. This was not so supernatural a way to live, yet it was necessary in order for them to develop into the mature people God wanted them to become. And if some of them, frightened of their new responsibilities, had attempted to return to the regime of the desert, we cannot suppose that the cloud and the manna would have returned. These belonged to an epoch that had ended.

There is of course real danger that the works and plans fabricated by man, instead of serving as the instrument of God, become a surrogate for him. This happened in Canaan, and it happens repeatedly today. The organization of prayer meetings, seminars and days of renewal can become enterprises more or less closed to grace. Those whose charism of leadership has been accepted by a community are tempted to use authority as a lever for imposing their own will. It is without a doubt indispensable for a maturing community to take care that the progressive institutionalization of its functions does not entail a loss of docility to the Spirit.

Nevertheless, if a community is to acquire depth, the challenge of growth cannot be evaded. The early stages of charismatic life, despite their loveliness, are also affected by superficiality, weakness and misdirection. Beginners inevitably place too much value on the charisms, even when they know in theory that the "fruits" of the Spirit are more important than the "gifts." They tend to measure the quality of prayer by the abundance of charismatic manifestations accompanying it. They suppose that spiritual growth is correlative with the profusion of miracles and wonders. They would like to be directed in all their actions by supernatural messages, or by biblical texts selected under divine inspiration, rather than to have recourse to common sense, reason, the lessons of experience, the wisdom of tradition, or the prescriptions of authority. They aspire to attain a state of such intimate contact with God that they will always know with certainty what he wants them to do. They expect to live in constant joy, out from under the shadow of the cross. The free, external expression of religious emotion, by singing, clapping, and enthusiastic shouts of praise, or prayer in tongues, becomes so identified in their minds with prayer in the Spirit that they have little appreciation for the values of silence and contemplation and almost no sense of depth and interiority. Feeling, emotion and experience hold too great a place in their esteem, to the detriment of faith, contemplation and service.

By gradually withdrawing some of the more external blessings, God gently re-educates us about what is truly substantial and enduring in the spiritual life: love, faith, humility, perseverance, and the like. Love, not joy, is its essence; faith, not experience, its foundation; humility, not spiritual power, the shield that protects it; perseverance under trials of all sorts is the test that proves, deepens and confirms it. Charismatic power, joy, harmony and experience have a real value in fostering this life, but when they are sought for their own sake, or cherished as dominant values, they deform and inhibit it. Perhaps the decisive issue confronting the charismatic renewal as it makes the transition from its early enthusiasm to a more sober mode of existence is how it will orient itself to the whole realm of enthusiasm: focus on it as a prime value to be perpetuated desperately by all available energies, or draw from it incentive for greater generosity and depth in the authentic life of the Spirit.

Need For A Charismatic Liturgy

Tom Holahan

James L. Empereur

Liturgy presupposes community. Liturgy is the articulation of the faith-experience of a particular Christian assembly. Worship is the self-image of the whole Christian community raised to the level of explicit communal activity. Liturgy is the ritual and symbolic bringing to visibility of the spirituality of the Church.

Such an understanding of Christian liturgy is now not only the possession of the liturgical theologian, but is also becoming the shared view of all Christians sensitive to the importance of worship. If this is the case, then it follows with inevitability that any viable and authentic liturgical situation will reflect the religious experience of those involved in the worship. If liturgy is to be the proclamation of the Church to the world that all secular values are worthwhile and can be salvific, then it must reflect the experiences of God that a particular people find in their ordinary lives.

With this kind of liturgical theology, anyone engaged in the planning of liturgy must take into consideration the

James Empereur, S.J. co-directs the Institute for Spirituality and Worship at Berkeley; he also serves as liturgy editor for *Folk Mass and Modern Liturgy Magazine.*

various ways in which God is working today to build up the Church. One of these ways is what is called the charismatic movement. Thus, this phenomenon of what is sometimes called "Catholic Pentecostalism" must find its expression in the liturgical worship of the Church. The hundreds of prayer meetings that have sprung up throughout this country during the last half-dozen years constitute a spiritual awakening that necessarily has repercussions for the liturgical movement.

If one maintains that liturgy is the cultic expression of the spirituality of Christians, then there should be such a thing as "charismatic liturgy." Any other kind of worship for a charismatic prayer group would be partial and lacking in authenticity.

The following description of a worshiping charismatic prayer group is fairly representative. Charismatic liturgies like any good liturgy start long before the actual celebration with the proper planning. The difference might be that charismatics have an actual prayer session in conjunction with their planning. Often the group will pray over the one chosen to be the celebrant.

Usually, charismatic celebrations are "played by the book," that is, there is little departure from the structure of the Roman rite. The music will often be the folk songs one hears in many parishes. However, only those songs which have a specific religious message are chosen. After the readings the response takes the form of the official texts plus prophecies, tongues and interpretation. The homily, which is often a shared one, may be followed by silence with occasional prophecies.

At the beginning of the liturgy of the Eucharist the participants gather around the altar and join in the offering by touching the vessels or laying their hands on the shoulders of those touching the vessels. After the liturgical, "Holy, Holy, Holy Lord," there may be a time of quiet praise in song. The sign of peace is usually a full embrace. After the distribution of communion there will be another period of praise as there was after the preface. This time can be filled with silence, tongues, interpretation and meditative song. In all these manifestations of praise, the celebrant determines how long each period will last and moderates the various charismatic expressions.

But the charismatic emphasis in contemporary liturgical spirituality is not the monopoly of those who have been "baptized in the Holy Spirit." There are elements in this movement that are important for non-charismatic liturgical contests. This should not be surprising since this is a spirituality in which the coming of the Holy Spirit as a personal and communitarian event is central. This continual experience of the Spirit allows one to proclaim that Jesus is the Lord. It is this basic religious experience and the way that it expresses itself in the lives and worship of the charismatic Christians that challenges us to examine what there is here that would be beneficial for the worship of all those who engage in specific Christian liturgy. To discover what these elements are, one must make an analysis of the charismatic prayer meeting.

Prayer meetings are long, lasting about two hours. They are a combination of introductory talks, spontaneous prayer and singing (frequently in tongues), prophecies, interpretations, a low murmur of prayer, prayers of petition and scriptural readings. In groups which are largely composed of Catholics, the prayer sessions frequently conclude with a eucharistic celebration. The purpose of these prayer meetings is the worship of God which will build up the body of Christ. There are several salient characteristics of these meetings which can be helpful in improving the parish liturgy as well as more specialized liturgical celebrations.

First, prayer meetings are local assemblies. The meeting is the expression of the community come together for prayer. These meetings are mostly composed of people who are regulars. This is important since a highly mobile population would make it difficult to create an atmosphere of faith, love and freedom in which the transcendent God can be experienced in a significant way. Only if there is a relatively stable group of those in whom the Spirit has been released will there be that situation which contributes to the building of the body of Christ.

What this says about liturgy is that it too must be local and concrete. It must be the focal point of a Christian community. The liturgy will be deficient if the community is not one in which there is some kind of personal relationship among the members. In the last analysis no amount of liturgical adaptation and experimentation can substitute for an ever present core of people who live and work together with some degree of faith sharing. And like the charismatic prayer meeting, the worshiping community not only reflects communal Christian experience, it also builds it up into the body of Christ.

Second, since charismatic prayer meetings are of varying sizes, they require different types of leadership. Small groups may require no specific leader while groups in the hundreds demand some very concrete leadership. Team leadership is not only a possibility but is greatly desired in some situations. Leadership in charismatic worship tends to be more democratic than is the case in traditional liturgies.

The liturgy also requires leadership. And the same principle should be operative here as is in the charismatic prayer sessions: no more leadership than is required. Small group liturgies require less leadership than the usual liturgical assembly. Hopefully, a democratized liturgical leadership will bring to an end the days of the domineering celebrant. Liturgical committees and teams are seen more and more as indispensable to good parish liturgy.

A third point is that the charismatics

expect that everyone at the prayer session will be active participants. If the charismatic local community is to grow, all must share as brothers and sisters in the Lord. It is redundant to emphasize that in the liturgy all should be willing participants, that there is no place for spectators. This is such a common understanding among those working in the renewal of worship that it has become a truism. Nevertheless, it is an important point on which the liturgical and charismatic movements are in complete agreement.

A fourth and major area of similarity between the prayer meeting and a lively and human liturgy are the many elements that go into making a prayer meeting. *Singing* the praises of the Lord is very important because it is singing as praise and worship and not singing for its own sake.

Likewise, music in official worship is for the purpose of heightening the liturgical experience. It is not for its own sake. Anything like concertizing would be foreign to the liturgy.

Worship is primary in the prayer meetings. God is the focus of all the prayers, the readings and the singing. The same must be affirmed about Christian liturgy. Anything else would be a distortion.

Prayer meetings are characterized by *love* and *affection*. One can see this in the enthusiasm with which the members participate in the meetings. *Joy* is another sign of the Spirit working in the group. This joy is not to be identified as a superficial frivolity, but is that about the prayer meetings which make them real and challenging.

Likewise, the Christian liturgical assembly should be characterized by love, affection and joy. Unfortunately, our present liturgical celebrations are too often without the kind of interpersonal communication expected by those united by the Gospel message. A joyous liturgy is one in which those who worship have their awareness of the mystery of God brought to greater concreteness and intensity.

Prayer meetings are pervaded with a sense of *peace*. At times because of personalities, there are feelings of tension and anxiety. But trust in the guidance of the Spirit as well as adequately trained leaders helps prevent anything that would hinder the participants' rest in God. At times things will take place that others do not understand. A truly charismatic community will respond to those situations with composure.

Peace should be a hallmark of Christian worship. If the peace of Christ is not present in our liturgy, we are dealing with a fragmented community where true worship is inhibited. One frequently experiences this alienation and lack of unity in churches where Catholics are uptight regarding the kiss of peace. Christians today must be more open to the Spirit and give of themselves, especially their bodies to the liturgy. If there is ever to be a liturgy which really reflects community, then there must be more ritual involvement on the part of all. But this entering into symbolic activity must be done without anxiety and a sense of uneasiness.

An important sign that a charismatic community is a healthy one is the *apostolic lives* of those involved. Charismatic leaders and theologians have expressed their concern over those communities which have become too introspective and do not have a sense of mission. If love for one another is to be Christian, it cannot remain within a group of like-minded people who are primarily preoccupied with their own relationship to Jesus.

A liturgy turned in on itself is inhibiting. Such a liturgy will atrophy and die. Liturgy means raised consciousness. It must sensitize us to the needs of others. Our worship-experience should impel us to give support to those who are in need of liberation.

Charismatics often point to the presence of *spiritual gifts* in the community as the sign of the operation of the Holy Spirit in the prayer meeting. These gifts are prophecy, interpretation and tongues. The purpose of these gifts in the community is the praise and worship of God. They are some of the ways that the Spirit has of building up the community and its prayer meetings. All charismatics are to be open to the reception of these gifts.

These same gifts can be an integral part of Christian liturgy. For instance, small group liturgies might well have the kind of reflections during moments of silence and free prayer which would qualify as prophecy and interpretation. However, what the charismatic prayer meeting has to say to traditional liturgy is not so much about the individual spiritual gifts, but that all worshipers (no matter what kind of liturgy) must be open to the presence and summons of the Holy Spirit.

Finally, what is so characteristic of all the prayer meetings is the *focus on God.* Whatever form the prayer session may take, it is not primarily a discussion group. It is time for men and women to come together to give praise for their union in God the Father.

Likewise the liturgy should not be ordered primarily for intellectual satisfaction. In our worship we must be careful that we are praising and thanking God in terms of our religious experience. We are not there to give information to each other. Even when care is taken that the liturgy is pervaded with an atmosphere of praise, it is necessary to avoid the excessive verbalism that deadens our contemporary liturgical practices. Those conducting and planning liturgies must not allow the liturgy of the Word to become so wordy and inflated as to derogate from the importance of the liturgy of the Eucharist.

The fifth and last point is that prayer meetings do not take place automatically. They demand a great deal of preparation. The one indispensable way to prepare for them is through the intensification of the personal lives of those who meet together. People who lead superficial lives will never contribute to a strong charismatic community. The spirit of prayer and the centrality of the love of God must shine through the community's prayer sessions. Intense spirituality here means an openness to receive from God what he calls one to as well as a readiness to give to others out of love. Prayer meetings are based on mutual support and encouragement.

Turning to the liturgy, it is almost trite to note that Christians must come to the liturgy with a sense of commitment and deep faith. Liturgy is not magic. It does not happen automatically either. It is the celebration of something already present, and in this case it is the community's faith and spirituality. All should have a sense of openness both to God and to their fellow Christians worshiping with them. Each liturgy can have something in particular to say to those present if they but listen. And in turn each worshiper can give of himself in love to others in response to the proclamation of Word and Eucharist. Only in this way will the liturgy be the paradigm of what the Church is all about in the world: the unambiguous sign of Christ indicating that God is drawing all mankind to himself wherever the humanization process is going forward.

These are some of the qualities of the charismatic movement which can be helpful for the renewal of the liturgy of the Church. Perhaps only in retrospect will the degree to which this movement has affected Christian liturgy be discernible. In any event, it is important that those working for the liturgical apostolate in the Church become acquainted with this important dimension of Christian spirituality. It more than anything else at the present time is restoring to our consciousness a sense of *praise* of God. And praise is what liturgy is all about. We should thank the Lord that the charismatic movement is once again re-emphasizing this feature for us and for the Christian community at large.

A PEOPLE OF HOPE

Rev. James J. Ferry
and The People of HOPE

"Since I prayed for the baptism in the Spirit during a Jesus Week I've been much more aware of God and the great love he has for each of us. I feel closer to him and can understand the gift of his Spirit as a further proof of his love for me. My prayer life has changed in that I praise and thank the Lord more than I've ever done before. I am just very grateful for the new power and strength that

James Ferry is a priest in the Archdiocese of Newark. Presently he serves as director of the House of Prayer Community and is a member of the Advisory Committee for the National Catholic Charismatic Renewal Conference.

has come into my life."

Baptism in the Spirit . . . praise . . . power . . . strength. Phrases and words like these, not too familiar to Catholics and other traditional Christians until recently, are being heard on university campuses, in family gatherings, in rectories and convents, from post-Vatican II liberals and conservatives alike.

Linda Fernandez, quoted above, has just finished her freshman year at St. Peter's College, Jersey City. She is perhaps typical of the young people who are searching—and finding—the "more" which makes the difference in their lives. The Jesus Week to which she refers was a six-day Week of Prayer in Christ the King parish, Jersey City, directed by a team, all members of our Christian community known as The People of HOPE.

The initials HOPE stand for House of Prayer Experience. In November 1970, in a country house in Stanfordville, New York, was laid the foundation of the first house of prayer strongly identified with the Catholic charismatic renewal. The current residential community of HOPE, numbering 26, lives in three houses located in Convent Station, New Jersey, Goshen, New York, and the innercity parish of Christ the King, Jersey City. There is also an extended, nonresidential group of more than 100 persons, including 26 married couples, who have asked to share as fully as they can the life of the HOPE community and are being trained to take increasing responsibility in varied evangelism programs such as the weeks of prayer described in this article.

We say that HOPE is a people living Christian community, sharing life on a deeper level than anyone of us has ever experienced before, and open to sharing what the Lord is doing among us with all who come with seeking hearts. Living in HOPE has taught us to trust in the Lord, to trust one another, and to trust the guidance of the Holy Spirit as he leads us, changes us, transforms us as disciples of Jesus who are learning first to live the Gospel and then to carry the Good News wherever he sends us.

How did we become involved in parish renewal programs? The answer is simply that we responded, after much prayer, to invitations of pastors to share what the Lord was teaching us about a life guided by the Holy Spirit, lived in a community centered in Jesus. We responded, too, to the hunger of God's people to hear with quickened faith and expectancy the Good News of God's love and saving power. We responded to their desire to know more about the new Pentecost for which Pope John prayed as he invited the contemporary Fathers of the Church to the Second Vatican Council: "Renew your wonders, Lord, as in a new Pentecost."

We experience a growing awe as priests, religious, laymen and laywomen share from the pulpits of parish churches the basic message of the

Gospel: that Jesus is alive and active in the power of his Holy Spirit today. Based on our contacts with thousands of persons who have come to Convent Station from nearly every state, from Canada, Italy, France, Belgium, Austria, Spain, Australia, Ireland, England, the Philippines, Africa, and Thailand, we are able to say with conviction that people all over the world are experiencing something new in their lives. There are few nations that have not felt the breath of the Spirit blowing gently but powerfully over the world, torn as it is by corruption and despair.

The people whose lives we have seen changed are people who were aware of God's love but are now experiencing a deeper capacity to respond to that love . . . people who never knew that the God they were trying to serve was a God who loved them personally . . . people who knew there was a God somewhere but not a God who was entirely for them . . . people who had never been to church in their lives and had never known God.

The "something new" is happening in the Catholic Church and in many Protestant churches through the charismatic renewal. In the words of Cardinal Suenens, "The '70s will be known in Church history as the beginning of the age of the Holy Spirit."

In October 1972 the HOPE community sponsored its first week of prayer in Englewood, New Jersey. Since that date HOPE has been responsible for eight weeks of prayer, sometimes referred to as Jesus Weeks, in parishes of the New York-New Jersey area. We could fill pages with letters received from people who attended these weeks of prayer. The effects on lives are going deeper as new prayer groups spring up in response to the urging of people whose lives were deeply touched, and prayer groups already in existence are increasing in membership. We quote here from a few of these letters.

On June 8 Rhonda Curtin, a Jewish woman, was received into the Catholic Church in Christ the King Church, Jersey City. It was the culmination of months of searching which she describes in the following paragraph:

"Ever since my husband Danny started going to prayer meetings, I wondered what the attraction was. I knew something good was happening in his life, but what and why? During the Jesus Week in Christ the King parish, which he attended every night, I went to meet him there early one evening, and that experience changed my life. I met people who talked of Jesus as a person who loved them, people who were happy and seemed at peace, people who spoke of spending time in prayer alone and together as one of the most important things they could do. I wanted to know *why*. As I listened, my heart was quickly filled by love of Jesus and by the gift of a faith I had never before experienced. That gift deepened and increased during the subsequent teaching received in the Life in the Spirit seminars which led to my being baptized in the Holy

Spirit. The next step was to receive instructions and to be received formally into the Catholic Church, to receive the sacraments of baptism and confirmation and, yes, finally to receive the Lord Jesus himself in the Eucharist. I praise God for his goodness to me and for the happy 'coincidence' that led me from a Jewish heritage to experience the fullness of God's promise in his Son Jesus."

Each week of prayer opens with a talk on the incredible love of God our Father who "loved the world so much that he gave his only Son, so that everyone who believes in him may not be lost but may have eternal life" (Jn. 3:16). Many people today are caught up in trying to earn God's love instead of receiving it as the free gift it is meant to be: "When the kindness and love of God our Savior appeared, he saved us. It was not because of any good works that we ourselves had done, but because of his own mercy that he saved us" (Tit. 3:4). God's love of his people *was, is,* and always *will be.* As St. Paul says in his letter to the Romans: "Neither death nor life . . . nothing that exists, nothing still to come . . . nor any created thing can ever come between us and the love of God made visible in Christ Jesus our Lord" (Rom. 8:38-39).

On the second night the talk is on repentance—the kind of repentance that brings life, new life, new joy, the basic repentance of turning away from serious sin and the on-going reorientation of our lives. Paul described it to the Ephesians: "You must put aside your old self. . . . Your mind must be renewed by a spiritual revolution, so that you can put on the new self that has been created in God's way" (Eph. 4:22-24).

The third talk is entitled "Accepting Jesus as Lord." When we realize that God loves us, his love enables us to turn away from sin and turn toward him. It is by accepting his love, accepting Jesus as our Lord, that we are transformed. The fact that Jesus *is* Lord is a lived experience; accepting his lordship on a day-to-day basis becomes a way of life. We were not meant to go through life trying to earn heaven or trying to take care of all our problems ourselves. Jesus wants us to be happy here and hereafter; he wants us to make him the center (Lord), and then he will give us the power to live fully, happily and peacefully, no matter what the circumstances of our lives.

Doug and Sue Ferrigno, parents of five children, attended a week of prayer in St. Mary's parish, Newburgh, New York. Doug explains their new life in the Spirit in this way:

"Our coming to Christ began when we attended a Jesus Week in our parish. Although we had begun to realize the need we had for a closer relationship with Jesus, going to a mission was out of character for us. Two thoughts expressed the first night kept us coming back. The first was: Who or what is really the Lord of your lives? We decided that our home, my job and Sue's

bridge and piano lessons were the center of our existence. Christ fit in on Sunday mornings only. The other key thought was: Repentance is merely a change of direction. The idea that God loves us and would help us change the direction of our lives was new to us. We didn't feel ready to pray for the baptism of the Holy Spirit at the end of the Jesus Week, but were ready to learn more, and learn we did, in a Life in the Spirit seminar at HOPE in Goshen, New York. Since our baptism in the Spirit, we are more and more living in the Spirit and truth of Jesus, and we are more and more experiencing the fruits of the Spirit, his peace, his joy, his love filling and overflowing all areas of our lives . . . our home, my job, our relationships with family and friends."

The fourth talk is woven around the gifts of the Spirit and what it means to be "baptized in the Holy Spirit." We are "children of a great promise" and the question we ask ourselves is whether we have heard the promise in our hearts and claimed that promise in our lives. In the words of Peter to the men of Jerusalem on Pentecost: "Turn away from your sins, each of you, and be baptized in the name of Jesus Christ, so that your sins will be forgiven, and you will receive God's gift, the Holy Spirit" (Acts 2:38).

The words of Jesus to the apostles, "Stay in the city until you are clothed with power from on high," are clarified in Acts 1:8: "You will receive power when the Holy Spirit comes on you, and then you will be my witnesses not only in Jerusalem but throughout Judea and Samaria, and indeed to the ends of the earth."

Being baptized in the Spirit means that we experience the release of the full power of the Spirit of Jesus in our daily lives. There are many manifestations of this power. The Word of God in Scripture comes alive in a new and deeper way and brings with it a new confidence and wisdom in being witnesses of the Lord. The charismatic gifts of which Paul speaks in 1 Corinthians 12 and 13—wisdom, knowledge, faith, healing, miracles, prophecy, discernment, tongues—are important for building up the body of Christ. But it is the fruits of the Spirit—love, joy, peace, patience—that change lives, our own first and then the lives of others. As we grow daily "living baptized in his Spirit," Christianity is more real and not just an ideal, the personal love of Jesus is experienced or deepened, and the words "Praise the Lord" become not a mere slogan but a way of life.

Carmine and Pat Ferragano of Oakland, New Jersey, were asked to give a witness to their new life in the Spirit during a Week of Prayer in St. Brendan's parish, Clifton, New Jersey. They wrote about their experience as follows:

"Although we had been involved in the charismatic renewal before the Jesus Weeks began, from time to time we would travel to a parish that was having a week of prayer. Each time we would listen, and each time the message would go deeper and deeper into the very fibers of our being, calling for

a response in us, a deeper surrender to the Lord. Then we were asked to share what the Lord had been doing in our lives. It was an opportunity to share with 300 strangers, which was quite a step of faith, and we rejoice that we had the opportunity to rely on the power of the Spirit. As we began to speak there was only joy, as if the Lord were saying to us, 'These are my special people, people uniquely my own, called here tonight. They are not strangers but my children; all of you are my children. These are your brothers and sisters.' The joy of being able to share from the pulpit how the Holy Spirit was guiding our everyday living was a humbling joy because we knew there must be more to Christianity than we had been living, and we rejoice that we were able to share the 'more' the Lord has given us through his Spirit."

Father Charles Reinbold of the parish of St. Joseph of the Palisades, West New York, New Jersey, describes the baptism of the Spirit as "one of the most spiritually supportive events of my life. . . . I feel that I have added power now through the Holy Spirit, and it also affects the people with whom I come in contact. The secret is yielding to the Lord. The more I do this, the more effective my ministry is. Through the charismatic experience, the Scriptures have become much more part of my life. My preaching has become more effective in this way. After Mass one day a woman came up to me and said, 'You speak with power.' I realized then that the Spirit was at work. As I rely more on the power of the Holy Spirit and less on myself, my ministry has become more effective."

On the fifth night, the talk is on "Healing the Whole Person." Healing is an important part of the mission of Jesus which he shared with his apostles: "He sent them forth to proclaim the kingdom of God and to heal. . . . So they set out and went from village to village proclaiming the Good News and healing everywhere" (Lk. 9:1, 6).

As we come to understand, believe and claim the power that God has given us through his Spirit, people are more and more experiencing healing in various ways. Since faith is beyond understanding, we know we need at times signs beyond our comprehension. Faith is moving mountains, mountains of spiritual sickness caused by sin that is healed each time we turn to the Lord Jesus in repentance—mountains of scars from hurts, self-pity, and painful experiences in the past as well as physical illnesses.

The Lord Jesus asks us to come to him in humility: "It is not the healthy that need the doctor but the sick. . . . I have come to call sinners. . . . Blessed are they who know their need of God. . . ." He asks us to come in faith to seek his love, his compassion and his power . . . to come with expectancy, to "ask, seek and knock" (Lk. 11:9) in submission to the will of his Father . . . to allow him to heal in us anything and everything that keeps us from experiencing his peace, his love and his joy in our lives.

In the simple words of Vickie Silverstadt:

"I had been searching for the reality of Jesus for years. I am a Catholic and I have tried to be a good wife, an understanding mother, a 'noble' widow and a compassionate neighbor. I cared for my aging parents, taught CCD, and served as lector at Mass. There were moments when Jesus was very real to me, but they were all too seldom. I wondered why I did not feel his presence more often; he seemed to elude me. Then one day, as I was reading the paper, I came upon an announcement of a Jesus Week in a nearby parish. Certainly if a week was to be devoted to Jesus, I would find some answers to my questions. I had a cold that week, but finally on the last day I was able to go. During the talk and subsequent prayer for healing, I found myself being gently healed and filled with the reality of Jesus. When I prayed for the baptism of the Holy Spirit, I definitely knew that I had just shed my 'old life' and was indeed reborn! My life has not been the same since. I look forward to the weekly prayer meetings and Life in the Spirit seminars where we are learning more and more of God's great love for us. Recently my son told me I had changed. 'You don't explode anymore. You ask questions first.' Praise God that the new me is visible where it has to show first, at home in my daily living."

For a long time HOPE has had a feeling that the Lord has a plan for New York. Father Tom Fenlon, a priest of the archdiocese of New York, shared the following personal reactions to the first charismatic mission in the New York archdiocese at St. Mary's, Newburgh, where he is assigned:

"'I feel like Nicodemus coming to Christ by night because of signs I see.' With these words I began the talk I gave during the Week of Prayer held at St. Mary's where I am assigned.

"The attendance at the evening and Sunday afternoon sessions ranged from 200 to 250 people; the Saturday afternoon talk attracted about 60 people, but I feel it was the highlight of the mission, for at the conclusion of the talk 36 people did go out two by two to visit homes around the church for several hours. What this did for them was remarkable; before going out most were fearful of what might happen, but they returned enthusiastic, eager to recount their experiences.

"As I said, I felt like Nicodemus when it came to the charismatic renewal. I have seen signs which have drawn me closer to it during the last three years, such as the joy which is evident in the prayer meetings or the deepening of faith of many formerly mediocre Catholics. Yet like Nicodemus who was afraid to go openly, things which held me back were a questioning of the speaking in tongues, a memory of the hostility of Spanish Pentecostals toward Catholics, and a feeling that it smacked of the 'old-time religion' which was strong on Jesus but very weak on social commitment.

"I have seen profound spiritual benefits in my life stemming from participation in the charismatic renewal: a greater awareness of prayer as praise of God which in turn has led me to want to sing forth the Gloria, Sanctus, and Agnus Dei at Mass. The psalms have a new freshness and vitality: they seem capable of expressing every mood I can feel. I sense a new boldness in preaching. While continuing to stress involvement in social concerns, I feel each of us must be more strongly grounded in Christ if we are not to become discouraged. I am no longer as reluctant to speak to individuals of what Christ can do in our lives as I once was."

Beyond all shadow of doubt, God is giving his people the new wine of life in Jesus through the power of the Holy Spirit. We are searching constantly now for new wineskins—elastic enough to be stretched to full capacity, light enough to be easily carried by a pilgrim people discipled and prepared by Jesus to evangelize, that is, call men to the Gospel, to live in the Spirit. We have to be detached, ready to move, lighthearted yet deeply centered in the Lord. His call demands much of us, but it carries with it the special joy of responding to the two invitations of Jesus: "Come, follow me; be my disciples. . . . Now, go, make disciples of all men."

We started with a House of Prayer. What the Lord has taught us in the House of Prayer has led us to become the people of HOPE. Prayer is an essential part of our lives but we have learned that prayer is not the answer. Jesus is. Gradually we have learned that God's plan revolves around Jesus, the Holy Spirit, Christian community and service. As we come to Jesus in the power of his Spirit, he builds us into a Christian community, a community eager to be of service—the service of being his witnesses.

We believe that the message of Jesus alive in the power of his Spirit is meant for all people, for we are all God's people—people who can claim the promise of his Spirit in our lives as we learn more and more to turn to the Lord Jesus, to trust him, to allow him to transform us, to allow the promise in John's Gospel that we would be "empowered to become children of God" (Jn. 1:12) to become a lived reality.

We are the people of HOPE, and our hope is in Jesus. As we come together we grow in knowing and experiencing the love of the Father so that we can more and more believe and proclaim that Jesus Christ is Lord to the glory of the Father. He is our hope of glory.

Restoring The Lordship Of Jesus

Harold F. Cohen

I have been involved in the charismatic movement since April 1969 and have been in a good position to watch its growth locally in New Orleans, nationally and internationally. Through speaking trips in the United States and abroad and through regional, national and international conferences, I have been able to be with a variety of groups and with most of the national leaders and with many of the international ones.

Harold Cohen, S.J. is an associate chaplain at Loyola University in New Orleans. He is a member of the National Service Committee of the Catholic Charismatic Renewal.

The following remarks are my personal views of what the charismatic experience means for individuals, for the Church, for Christianity and for society at large. (The charismatic movement, like any other, has its concomitant problems—witness the problems in the early Church in the decades after Pentecost as mentioned in Acts and Paul's letters. While in no way denying these, I am focusing on the positive.)

The charismatic movement in the Catholic Church began at Duquesne University in Pittsburgh. In 1966 a group of lay professors began praying to the Holy Spirit for a deeper Christian life. At the beginning of 1967 they were prayed with at an interdenominational prayer group in Pittsburgh for a fuller life in the Holy Spirit and indeed began to experience such a life. Soon after this, in February 1967, one of this group was among the organizers of a retreat for a group of college students. On this retreat, the students experienced in a new way the presence and love of God in their lives. On returning to campus, without knowing it, they were the first charismatic prayer group in the Catholic Church. They began "stumbling" into charismatic gifts. Manifestations of the Spirit which are written about in Scripture but which they had never experienced personally began to crop up among them. From this group the charismatic movement spread to other campuses and then around the country and is now a rapidly growing movement in the whole Catholic Church.

The initial experience of charismatics is frequently called "baptism in the Holy Spirit." (The word *experience* can be misleading. The beginning of this fuller release of the Spirit can be very gentle with little or no accompanying emotions.) This expression in its verb form, *to be baptized* in the Holy Spirit, is found in all the Gospels and in Acts (Mt. 3:11; Mk. 1:8; Lk. 3:16; Jn. 1:33; Acts 1:5; 11:16). Probably the most common view among Catholic theologians is that *baptism in the Holy Spirit is a fuller release of the love and power of the Holy Spirit, already received in baptism, confirmation (and orders), in an individual's personal and apostolic life.*

To sum up the fruit of this experience, I would say that it is the renewal and/or restoration of the lordship of Jesus Christ in individuals and, through them, in the Church, the churches and society. I will expand on each of these areas.

Individuals. The lordship of Jesus is being renewed and restored in individuals as they come to know Jesus Christ in a close personal way: as their *Savior* to whom they come in conversion and repentance; as their *Lord* to whom they come in total commitment; as the *Christ*, the *anointed anointer*, who gives them a fuller life in the Spirit and calls them to lay their whole lives before him to use as he wills. They experience a greater desire for private prayer and prayer with their brothers and sisters. They experience a growing union with the Father, Jesus and the Spirit in their daily lives. They begin to enjoy reading Scripture and often spend much time doing so.

As the lordship of Jesus is restored in their lives, they begin to experience the need to grow in this relationship together with other Christians. The phenomenon of rapid growth of prayer groups and prayer communities is a result of this. But the experience of community spills over from the prayer groups into the daily lives of people. They share their love of the Lord, their faith-life, their needs and concerns. The liturgy becomes the worship, not of a group of isolated individuals or families, but of a united community. Prejudices begin to wither as concern for others grows. I believe that from this seed of concern much social action will develop.

Charismatics are not only experiencing the lordship of Jesus but are giving witness to this. We have looked upon confirmation as the sacrament especially enabling us to witness to Christ, yet most Catholics seem to do little of this. When the Spirit comes in a fuller way, it begins to happen in fact: "You will receive power when the Holy Spirit comes on you, and then you will be my witnesses" (Acts 1:8). I hope that the bishops at the fall Synod on Evangelization will study the actuality of this in the charismatic movement.

The lordship of Jesus is also being restored in their lives through the presence of the charismatic gifts. The gift or ministry of each person is a specification of his vocation in the Church. He is sanctified in living out his calling through the exercise of his gifts; others are sanctified by his ministry. It is this dimension which most often causes problems to people outside of the movement and yet it is this very dimension that manifests the presence and love of God in our midst. The charismatic dimension of his Church was stressed by Jesus (Mk. 3:13-14; 16:15-20; Lk. 9:1-2; 10:1, 8-9) and lived out in the lives of his early followers (throughout Acts; Rom. 12:3-8; 1 Cor. 12—14; Eph. 4:4-16; 1 Pt. 4:10-11). Vatican II in its document on the Church stressed that it is not only through the hierarchy and the sacraments but also through the charismatic gifts that the Spirit sanctifies his people. In its document on the apostolate of the laity, the Council stressed the importance of the use of these gifts by each member of the body of Christ.

This dimension has always been in the Church as is attested to in the lives of the saints, the presence in our midst of shrines like Guadalupe, Lourdes and Fatima, and as lived out in the simple faith of people who in their prayers and novenas have expected God to respond in an extraordinary way. I like to think of the Church as a large magnolia tree which has always had its charismatic flowers but which, when the breath of the Spirit brings a new springtime, blossoms out in new and greater profusion. I feel that now we are at the end of winter and the beginning of a great new springtime in the Church. The charismatic gifts are a sign of the presence and love of the Lord calling his people to himself.

Pope Paul has significantly commented on these fruits of the charismatic renewal: "Certain common notes appear in this renewal: the taste for deep prayer, personal and in groups, a return to contemplation and an emphasizing of praise of God, the desire to devote oneself completely to Christ, a great availability for the calls of the Holy Spirit, more assiduous reading of Scripture, generous brotherly devotion, the will to make a contribution to the service of the Church. *In all that, we can recognize the mysterious and discreet work of the Spirit, who is the soul of the Church*" (*L'Osservatore Romano*, October 11, 1973; italics added).

The Restoration of the Lordship of Jesus in the Church. I like to pray on the levee of the Mississippi, and I see that the current in the middle of the river is much swifter than the current at the sides. I look upon the charismatic movement in the Church today as a strong current blown along by the wind of the Spirit which is meant to widen out and catch up the whole river in a swifter flow. I don't see all in the Church as called to the movement, but I do see all as called to be in a renewed and restored Church whose Lord is truly Jesus Christ manifested in the presence and activity of his Spirit.

Charismatics often compare this movement to the liturgical movement. For many years it proposed liturgical changes; once these changes were adopted by Vatican II, it ceased to exist as a strong movement. Likewise I feel that the charismatic movement is an instrument of God to renew the whole Church and that once the Church is renewed the charismatic movement as a movement will cease to exist.

The specific way in which the Spirit is restoring the reality of the lordship of Jesus in his Church is, I believe, through restoring the ministries of Jesus to their full strength.

The first of these is the ministry of prophecy. (Cf. *Riding the Wind* by George T. Montague, S.M., Word of Life, 1974.) The main prophetic message of the charismatic movement is the message of the Book of Consolation of Isaiah: "Console my people, console them, says your God. . . . Here is the Lord Yahweh coming with power, his arms subduing all things to him; he is like a shepherd feeding his flock, gathering lambs in his arms, holding them against his breast" (Is. 40:1, 10-11). "See, I am doing a new thing; I am putting water in the wilderness to give my chosen people drink; the people I have formed for myself will sing my praises" (Is. 43:19-21). The Lord through this outpouring of the Spirit is calling his children back to himself no matter how far they have strayed from him.

The second message of the charismatic renewal is that of Psalm 127: "Unless the Lord builds the house, those who build it labor in vain." The Lord is calling us to realize that the work of renewal is his work. We must seek his guidance in daily prayer and in the community of our fellow Christians. Too often in the Church today we have slipped into a secular humanism, acting and thinking as if the renewal of the Church were primarily *our* work and not God's. We must, like Paul, seek *his* strength: "For this I toil, striving with all the energy which he mightily inspires within me" (Col. 1:29).

Evangelization. Through this ministry the charismatic movement is proclaiming the basic Gospel message of conversion to Jesus the Savior, commitment to Jesus the Lord, openness to Jesus the Anointer. This basic message has to be preached and appropriated as the foundation on which all the further teaching and activity of the Church must be built. By presupposing this foundation we have often built on sand. (Cf. *Unless the Lord Build the House* by Ralph Martin, Ave Maria Press, 1971.)

Healing and Deliverance. Jesus' teaching and preaching were accompanied by the healing of the sick and casting out of devils. The message of his saving love was incarnate in his saving power. Jesus was not an abstract Savior; his Father's love was not a theoretical thing. The love of the Father and the saving power of Jesus were seen and felt: the blind saw, the deaf heard, the lame walked, the dead were raised to life. Peter sums up the public ministry of Jesus: "God had anointed him with the Holy Spirit and with power, and because God was with him, Jesus went about doing good and curing all who had fallen into the power of the devil" (Acts 10:38). (Cf. *Healing* by Francis MacNutt, O.P., Ave Maria Press, 1974.)

When Jesus sent out his apostles and disciples, he sent them out not only to preach the Good News but with power to confirm it through healing and deliverance (Mk. 3:13-14; 15:15-20; Lk. 9:1-2; 10:1, 8-9). The apostles and early Christians lived this out; they knew of no dichotomy between proclaiming the message and confirming it with signs and wonders: "And now, Lord, take note of their threats and help your servants to proclaim your message with all boldness, by stretching out your hand to heal and to work miracles and marvels through the name of your holy servant Jesus" (Acts 4:29-30).

I believe one reason why the Christian message is so often sterile today is that it is not being preached in the power of the Spirit. We have put a false separation between the teaching-preaching ministry of Jesus and his ministry of healing and deliverance. As Christians come again to experience the loving presence of Jesus in their midst through his gentle touch in healing and deliverance, the message will no longer seem irrelevant; God will no longer seem somewhere out there if not altogether dead.

As our experience of the healing power of Jesus grows, we will have less of the strange phenomenon of some members of the Church wondering if God intervenes directly in human life and other members of the same Church experiencing his loving intervention daily.

As our recognition of the power of the evil one and evil spirits grows, we hopefully won't have the sad reoccurrence of an address like Pope Paul's "Deliver Us from Evil" (*L'Osservatore Romano*, November 23, 1972), looked upon by some as a harkening back to medieval times. Rather, the reality of Christ's victory over Satan will be applied through the deliverance ministry to bring about the full liberation that Jesus came to give us.

Teaching. There are so many things the charismatic movement is teaching to its members and through them to the Church that all I can do is briefly mention them. It is teaching the importance of the charismatic dimension in the Church today. This is not peripheral to Christianity but at the very heart of the Church in her mission to proclaim the lordship of Jesus. Ramifications of this are many. The main role of bishops and pastors is that of discerning the gifts and ministries given by the Spirit to their people and priests, and of calling forth these gifts and ministries to be used for the building up of the body of Christ. The community dimension of Christianity is closely related to this. The movement is underlining the need to remodel our parishes. Some sort of small subcommunity structure is needed where every Christian can experience the love and concern of his brothers and sisters and receive pastoral ministry through them. Priests simply do not have the time to give to every person, but every member of the parish has his gift with which to minister to others. It is teaching us to look for ministers in the Church not simply on the basis of their experiencing a call but also on the basis of their ministry's having been tested and confirmed by its fruits in the people of God. The movement is teaching the importance of total commitment to Jesus (not simply the acceptance of dogmatic truths) in the preparation for baptism and confirmation. It is teaching us the tremendous power in the sacraments: the healing power of Jesus in the Eucharist who comes to transform our lives; the power of inner healing that Jesus wants to be exercised in the context of the sacrament of reconciliation. The Lord wants not only to forgive men's sins but to heal the roots of those sins, the roots that often keep people in a kind of psychological slavery to one kind of habit or another. It is teaching us the healing power in the anointing of the sick (as is brought out in the new rite). It is emphasizing the importance of true obedience to authority in the Church today. The charismatic renewal, a predominantly lay movement, by and large has no anticlerical spirit, but quite the contrary. The attitude of national leaders is one of collaborating with the bishops as their shepherds in the Lord and not apart from them. Finally it is demonstrating the beauty of praise-filled worship such as is mentioned in Vatican II's document on the liturgy. As Cardinal Suenens puts it, we are ceasing to be God's frozen people and beginning again to be his chosen people.

Intercessor. The charismatic movement is rediscovering the power of intercessory prayer and fasting. Through the prayers and sacrifices of many, local parishes and dioceses will be transformed.

Servant. Like Jesus the charismatic movement is called to be a servant of the whole Church. (Often we are accused of being elitist. I think that this impression is taken by people who translate enthusiasm into a holier-than-thou attitude. My own experience is that charismatics do not think they are holier or better than others. They simply want to share their blessings.) This call to be servant is being exercised by many people in the renewal as they take on works of service in their parishes such as teaching in the CCD program, working in the liturgy program, and working on the parish council. Following Steve Clark of Ann Arbor, I exhort charismatics to be ready to do humble, unattractive work in parishes so that like Jesus we can wash the feet of our brothers.

Peacemaker. In the charismatic renewal many gaps are being bridged: between generations, between blacks and whites, between liberals and conservatives. This ministry of peacemaking is one that will be exercised more and more in the whole Church, reconciling divisions that now tear us apart. In the power of the Spirit we can all be one.

As these ministries of Jesus (prophecy, evangelization, healing and deliverance, teaching, interceding, serving and reconciling) are restored to their full strength in the Church, his lordship will be re-established among his people.

The Restoration of the Lordship of Jesus in the Churches. Christianity today is often looked upon as flowing in three main rivers—Catholicism, Protestantism, and Pentecostalism—though Orthodox Christianity could certainly be considered as a fourth. In each of these rivers today there is a faster-flowing current—the renewal which the Holy Spirit is bringing about. (In the Pentecostal churches which have been responsible for bringing the renewed emphasis and experience of the charismatic gifts of the Spirit to Protestants and Catholics there can be a need for renewal. Like the rest of us they can sink into ritual in place of love.) As these rivers in Christianity are renewed by this powerful current of the Holy Spirit widening out within them they will be brought to a fuller realization of the lordship of Jesus. Once Jesus is Lord of the totality of each of these churches, *he* can bring them together. I share Cardinal Suenens' hope that as this millennium has been one of disunity, the next will be one of unity.

The words of the fathers of Vatican II in their document on ecumenism are pertinent here: "This most sacred synod urgently desires that the initiative of the sons of the Catholic Church, joined with those of the separated brethren, go forward without obstructing the ways of divine providence and without prejudging the future inspirations of the Holy Spirit.

Further, this Synod declares its realization that the holy task of reconciling all Christians in the unity of the one and only Church of Christ transcends human energies and abilities. *It therefore places its hope entirely in the prayer of Christ for the Church, and the love of the Father for us, and in the power of the Holy Spirit.* 'And hope does not disappoint, because the charity of God is poured forth in our hearts by the Holy Spirit who has been given to us' (Rom. 5:5)." (Italics added)

The Restoration of the Lordship of Jesus in Society. In God's providence I feel Pope Leo XIII has shown us the way to the Christianization of the world. Leo XIII is perhaps best known today for his encyclical *Rerum Novarum* on the condition of the working classes. But he also wrote the encyclical *Divinum Illud* on the Holy Spirit. He ended this encyclical asking the faithful to pray with our Lady that God would send forth his Spirit to renew the face of the earth with signs and wonders.

His papacy, which spanned the end of the 19th century and the beginning of the 20th, points out to us God's direction in renewing his Church and the world: God will renew us by giving us great faith in the power of his Holy Spirit and a true concern for all the needs of our brothers.

The Episcopalian Church of the Redeemer in Houston is the best model I know of an individual parish that exhibits this faith and this concern. It blends reverent worship, on-going instruction in the Christian life, and true outreach to the social needs in their area.

The charismatic renewal in the Catholic Church is in its infancy. As we grow in maturity, I feel the Spirit will lead us (in his way and in his time) to reach out to our brothers and sisters and reform those structures of society that hold them in oppression today. As the churches, and ultimately the one Church after we've all been united, reach out in the love and power of the Spirit to mankind, the lordship of Jesus will truly be restored to the whole world.

To try to summarize what I have written: the charismatic movement is a movement of renewal and reconciliation. Jesus said: "When I am lifted up from the earth, I shall draw all men to myself" (Jn. 12:32). I see the Spirit today lifting up Jesus to the glory of God the Father (cf. Phil. 2:11). As Jesus is lifted up he is drawing all to himself. As he unites men to himself, he unites them with one another.

The charismatic movement is, I feel, a sovereign act of God the Father restoring the lordship of Jesus in the power and love of the Holy Spirit in individuals, in the Church, in the churches and in society.

"Glory be to him whose power, working in us, can do infinitely more than we can ask or imagine; glory be to him from generation to generation in the Church and in Christ Jesus forever and ever. Amen" (Eph. 3:20-21).

IGNATIUS HOUSE: An Experiment In Pentecostal Community

Terry Malone

"Why are they so happy?" is probably the most common reaction registered when people come into contact with the Ignatius House charismatic prayer community in Rutherford, N.J.

Rick Smolan

It isn't only the effect of an exuberant prayer meeting, which is often a person's first encounter with the group. Rather, as one meets the members under other circumstances it becomes clearer that the quality of their relationships with one another—marked by gentleness, attentiveness, respect, warmth and affection—provides the attraction.

It was this quality that formed Ignatius House Community (IHC) and which will probably sustain it through changes in its structure and focus. It is also the quality which holds the most importance for the Church and society.

For clarity's sake, the first part of this article outlines the face of the community: membership, structure, spirituality, focus. The second part attempts to explore and raise some questions about its potential effect.

Terry Malone is a journalist writing for *The Advocate.* She was associated with Ignatius House for three years.

The term "community" or IHC refers to observations made of the group as a whole, particularly when assembled for prayer, teachings or meetings, while observations referring to individuals are so indicated.

Not all the observations made here are necessarily applicable to other charismatic groups. But they—as well as any Christian group—can benefit from the questions.

When IHC began taking shape in 1971, it was characterized by the natural warmth that flowed from three dozen young people who enjoyed spending time together at prayer meetings, Mass, Monopoly games or talking. That early spirit hasn't dimmed with growth in number, but now it flows from a more conscious effort to "love one another."

Ignatius House Community (drawing its name from the Newman Center at Fairleigh Dickinson University, Rutherford, where the early prayer meetings began in 1969) is a "covenant" community. This means that members formally agree to commit themselves to God and one another through prayer, study, community and apostolic action, reordering their priorities (especially time and finance) toward that end.

Today some 130 people belong to the community, about a third having signed the covenant and the remainder preparing to do so. Most are young, late teens to mid-20s, and single. A dozen marriages have taken place in the community, and there are as many infant to pre-school children growing up in IHC.

Members represent all economic and social backgrounds: MA's and dropouts, professionals and clerks, some coming from the drug culture, others from convents and seminaries. Most have had exposure to Catholic thought in Catholic schools or CCD, but for many it is their first experience of living their faith.

The effect the covenant relationship has had in the three years since it was incorporated has been to form a community with a twofold purpose: development of a strong, cohesive unit, and an evangelistic outreach. As a means of fostering both, the community has developed a structure, on the basis that order is a means of "facilitating love," providing time and opportunities for people to get to know one another.

In households, for example, members share expenses and responsibilities in the house, meet two to three times a day for common prayer, eat meals in common, and meet formally once a week to talk and pray. About a dozen such households are located in Rutherford, a suburban area minutes from New York City. They are comprised of from two to a dozen people, mostly single men or women, although some combine married couples (particularly families) with singles.

For those whose circumstances don't permit them to live in a household, "subgroups" also meet weekly to pray, share a meal, and talk. Some members choose to live in "Christian apartments" which simply do not include the structure or schedule of a household.

The community comes together for Mass and prayer each Sunday, and so that activities can run smoothly, meetings are held frequently for various ministries: prophecy, child care, evangelism, music, and internal administration.

Another type of order is maintained in the community through a diffused system of pastoral care, or personal concern and guidance. It's headed by four "shepherds": a priest, layman and a married couple who chose the term in preference to "overall coordinators" because they felt it conveyed more accurately the kind of care with which they wanted to exercise their ministry.

Unit coordinators care for the heads of households and subgroups, who in turn care for the individuals in those groups. In addition to these, ministry heads have pastoral care for the people in their ministries.

IHC is primarily a praying, spiritual community, containing a pervasive sense of God's active presence in daily life. He is naturally a part of conversation, prayers at meals, meetings, and even parties.

One's personal prayer life is seen as essential to the life of the community, while shared prayer is intended to support and strengthen one another.

Personal prayer, for most, means a deep interior life. It is meditative, even contemplative, a time of inner quiet balanced by the use of vocal prayer, reading and use of the prayer charisms. Members pray about major decisions and a multitude of minor ones, often asking others to help them discern God's will in various situations.

A dozen men and women are earnestly considering a vocation to celibacy —not as a religious, but within the framework of IHC.

Community prayer centers on Scripture and the Eucharist. The tone ranges from hushed and relective, with deep silences, to exuberantly joyful; it is sometimes serious, rarely somber, always reverent.

At this stage, because most of its energies are poured into the internal growth of the community—prayer, relationships, and ministries—IHC appears turned in on itself.

Charismatic renewal in general receives criticism for its lack of social outreach—however that may be defined.

If one looks for a community organized for a social cause, he won't find it in IHC. Nor will he find a community involved in an already organized cause. Individual volunteers number only a handful.

But what has happened because of the emphasis on self-development is the creation of an environment in which the traditional corporal works of mercy are a way of life, forming a warm and caring spirit of generosity. Not only is this widespread in the community—to name a few: home repairs, babysitting, financial assistance—it overflows to guests who want to learn about the community, and to strangers who stumble in, needing shelter, food, and sometimes clothing.

Also, evolving naturally from its spiritual origins and development, the community has its own special brand of outreach: evangelism, which is integrated into the whole of community life.

For example, the thrust of the weekly prayer meeting (separate from the community meeting) is God's love, personal conversion and commitment. Newcomers are warmly greeted and introduced to charismatic renewal and the community before the prayer meeting. A two-month-long, weekly seminar prepares them for the baptism of the Spirit if they request it. There are also weekly workshops on Scripture and Christian growth.

Following the prayer meeting, some community members staff the "Jesus room" where people can go to talk or pray about their personal commitment to Christ. Others are available in the "prayer room" where people can pray for specific intentions. (The prayer room seems to be developing an important outreach, as people seem to find great support in others praying for them. The intentions run the gamut from "my uncle who's sick" to individuals seeking prayer for themselves for personal difficulties, troubled relationships, emotional problems.)

Other members share informally on a "getting to know you" basis. The community's rock band, "The Joyful Noise," blends Gospel rock with teaching, informal sharing and witnessing, and an invitation to those present to "let Jesus in" to their lives. They reach out not only through the community's coffeehouse, but by request at various churches.

Some members practice "direct evangelism" (the "God loves you and has a plan for your life" variety) either in an organized way (the university dorms, for example) or spontaneously with people they meet. For the most part however, it is indirect, a witness of their lifestyle and the way they relate. Happiness makes people wonder.

Therefore, insofar as social outreach is concerned, the problem is not that Ignatius House Community has none. By its evangelism it offers relief for modern man's hunger for meaning, and in its brand of evangelism offers a dimension of the Christian life that perhaps a social action group may not. Both are vital members in the whole body of Christ. Moreover, there is some validity to the community's reasoning that people must change before society can. The problem is, however, that social awareness is lacking, and that seems to be a symptom of a much deeper flaw.

One notices that individuals as a rule do not talk much about the world community, or even about the larger Church community except where it applies to charismatic renewal. If there is in fact individual consciousness of the world, it does not find expression when the community is together, not in teachings or prayer. In fact, the overall scope of the community is limited.

Explore, for example, these areas: content and presentation of teaching, lack of dialogue, suppression of dissent, and over-emphasis on the spiritual.

Although the teaching's basic source is Scripture (and a relief from the watered-down Gospel often encountered elsewhere), it lacks a broadening outlook. Rarely, if ever, are contemporary theologians mentioned. Nor is there any consideration given to crucial contemporary issues that call for Christian response: medical ethics, government and politics, racism, women's rights, sexual mores.

While members live up to the prayer, community and action (evangelism) aspects of the covenant, the study phase seems to be neglected. Members talk about their "spiritual reading," but one does not hear much reference to critical study (even though the small community library has such works).

Books available at the prayer meeting are largely the works of Catholic and Protestant Pentecostals. Teachers and guest speakers are figures in charismatic renewal, with most teachings given by individuals in the community.

Teachings are presented in a tone of certainty, lecture-style, with an authoritative note common to charismatic renewal: "The Lord's word to us is. . . ." "The Lord's plan for us is. . . ." "The Lord is calling us to. . . ."

Also, the basic Gospel message is not made that distinct from its application to community life, and however unintentional that may be, it tends to infer that IHC (or at least the charismatic community) is the only viable place in which to experience Christianity.

Reinforcing limited content and restrictive presentation is the fact that there is no room for discussion following teachings (with the exception of one or two community weekends given during the year in which group discussions are held). Members are urged to discuss with their households or subgroups—but that's like telling a student to discuss his lessons after school: the spontaneity and vitality of the learning experience is lessened, if not eliminated.

When disagreement is the issue, restrictions are even stronger. Members are asked not to discuss their negative feelings with one another, but to bring them to the shepherds. The reason given for this is that negativism is destructive to the unity which is seen as essential if the community is to survive. Therefore, whatever promotes unity is acceptable, whatever rocks it is not.

The community seems wary of confrontation or challenge to its views; it doesn't seem to give these due credit as being positive tools for growth. Members are taught about submission and authority, but not enough attention is given to the right to question authority.

In reality a number of individuals bring their complaints to the shepherds, but still this is weak on three counts:

1. Expression of different viewpoints (particularly negative ones) only to leaders gives an individual a limited audience from which to gain insight.

2. It robs the rest of the community of the challenge of examining an issue from another view, even if that view is incorrect.

3. Perhaps most importantly, it raises a question about the quality and validity of the unity the community claims: How authentic is a love which does not learn how to listen to one another's disagreements, negativism or opinions? Is unity the result of corralling dissent, or of learning to listen to it and learn from it maturely, together?

Members have a say when decisions have to be made, insofar as they provide feedback. (Households and subgroups discuss an issue, and the heads provide feedback to the shepherds, who make the final decision.) Even so, the satisfaction, support, challenge and broadening of one's ideas by others is limited.

Another restricted area is the spiritual focus of IHC, because although creating a strong sense of the presence of God, it seems to have sidestepped the human element.

One often hears, for example, "we are called to. . . ." with little acceptance or recognition of "where we are at." It seems to be more of a strain to become, rather than a patience with becoming.

Granted, people need the ideal before them to remind them of what they can become. But emphasis on the ideal is constant, and somehow negatively implies that where one is at is not OK.

It is frustrating, too, to be striving so much for the ideal when by comparison so little recognition is given to the assortment of human needs and problems that need to be dealt with patiently, or even to the human worth and potential that needs affirmation occasionally.

This restrictedness is detrimental precisely because it is restrictive: it does not allow for balanced growth and is, in fact, reminiscent of spoon-fed Christianity.

A focus that is so restricted to this one type of faith experience will certainly reinforce it, but won't challenge or broaden it. It is certainly not conducive to social awareness.

The community needs to recognize—perhaps much of charismatic renewal does, too—to what it is simply filling people's needs for security and certainty, and to what extent it is challenging them to grow. It needs to ask if it is actually stimulating renewal and change, or producing a new Christian ghetto.

The community could stand to expand its teachings with 20th-century Christian views, encourage open questioning and scholarship, draw on the resources available outside charismatic renewal (diocesan agencies and programs, for example), and explore Christian humanism a little more. It would benefit from some form of regular informal rap sessions, not only to air grievances but to simply learn from one another in a way that is not provided in households or sub-groups.

Perhaps this concentration on itself is a necessary, temporary phase of the community's growth, in much the same way that a child needs to focus on himself to establish his identity before he begins exploring the people and the world around him.

One would hope so. For there is a core to the life of the community that deserves to be liberated, encouraged and challenged: the individual freedom of people who choose to believe in a personal and loving God and to consciously invite him to take part in their lives; the power of that kind of faith: not only that God can do all things, but that he will, in big matters and small; the desire to love, and the willingness to wade through years of emotional and cultural blockage to do so.

There is power in that core of freedom, faith and will. And after observation of the community over a period of three years, it is clearly that power which has effected the change in the way people relate to one another.

The witness of a common lifestyle is secondary. Besides, not everyone can be expected to develop his full potential in that kind of intensive communal life. But it is the basic relationship aspect of IHC which challenges the Church to distinguish between a spirit of community, and a community based on deep commitment of one person to another. It is that which challenges society by providing an alternative to the alienation and fear that marks it and keeps individuals isolated.

That's why one hopes this "restricted" phase of Ignatius House Commuty's growth is a temporary one, a growing pain. Because if it is truly the direction the community is taking, the narrow scope and spoon-fed formation are potentially fertile ground for the development of passive, narrow-minded Christians, which could be destructive of the very power which gives the community life.

Filled With New Wine

J. Rodman Williams

In this review article I will mention several books that have appeared in the last two or three years which give a variety of approaches to the pentecostal/charismatic renewal. I shall by no means attempt to cover the field, especially since the literature is so rapidly increasing.

J. Rodman Williams is an educator and president of the International Charismatic Communion of Presbyterian Ministers. His books on charismatic renewal include *The Era of the Spirit* **and** *The Pentecostal Reality.*

The best single introduction undoubtedly is the volume entitled *The Pentecostals: The Charismatic Movement in the Churches* (Minneapolis: Augsburg, 1972) by Walter J. Hollenweger. Dr. Hollenweger, formerly a Swiss Pentecostal preacher, later Secretary of the Division of World Mission and Evangelism of the World Council of Churches, and now professor of Missions at the University of Birmingham, England, has produced an encyclopedic survey that investigates the history, beliefs, and practice of Pentecostal churches throughout the world. Also there is a brief survey in the opening chapter of the charismatic movement in the historic churches with particular reference to the recent renewal in the Roman Catholic Church. Though I find myself differing with some of Hollenweger's theological assessments, the book is invaluable for understanding the contemporary scene.

For the reader who desires to go more deeply into American backgrounds of the contemporary charismatic renewal, *The Holiness-Pentecostal Movement in the United States* (Grand Rapids: Eerdmans, 1971) by Vinson Synan is very helpful. One will find in this scholarly volume (Dr. Synan is chairman of the Division of Social and Behavioral Sciences at Emmanuel College in Georgia) no apologia for any one position but a very readable and informative analysis of the history of the Holiness-Pentecostal movement together with a fine discussion and analysis of its accomplishments.

Moving now to a book that deals particularly with the contemporary renewal, I refer the reader to *The Holy Spirit in Today's Church: A Handbook of the New Pentecostalism* (Nashville: Abingdon, 1973) by Erling Jorstad. Professor Jorstad, historian at St. Olaf's College, Minnesota, in this important handbook has sought to bring together historical background and contemporary source material that will enable the reader to judge for himself the significance of the present charismatic renewal. After a brief historical survey Professor Horstad summarizes some of the controversy that has arisen over "the new Pentecostalism." This is followed by a series of chapters that include excerpts from various charismatic and non-charismatic writers on such subjects as "Prayer Meetings," "Baptism in the Spirit," "Speaking in Tongues," and "The Gift of Healing," Quotations are to be found from those within the renewal, such as Larry Christenson, Dennis Bennett, Don Basham, Fr. Edward O'Connor, Fr. Donald Gelpi, Jim Cavnar, and Kevin and Dorothy Ranaghan. Also the critical voices of persons such as Anthony Hoekma, William Criswell, and J. Daniel Joyce are heard. On the whole the book reflects a cautious pro-charismatic stance.

From this reviewer's perspective the best recent single volume on the charismatic renewal is that entitled *Filled with New Wine: The Charismatic Renewal of the Church* (New York: Harper, 1974) by James W. Jones. Dr. Jones, an ordained Episcopal clergyman and professor of religion at Rutgers University, writes as one deeply committed to the movement but also with a keen sense of questions frequently raised. In the preface Jones writes: "Many in the traditional churches are perplexed by what they read about Pentecostals; many are turned off by what they hear. This book is written for just such an audience." Jones makes a strong case for the charismatic renewal as a God-given answer to the hunger of people for the basic experiences of Christianity, and holds that this renewal signifies the rebirth of the church in the twentieth century. The Pentecostal experience "fulfills and carries forward our baptism, our confirmation, our life of sacrament and service. . . . It is a strengthening and fulfilling of one's life in Christ." It is a renewal of Christian community whereby "the church is made into the body of Christ." Further, "the charismatic movement is *the* ecumenical movement, not because it is creating structural alignments (it isn't), but because it is bringing into being a new sense of the common life of the people of God." The climax of this renewal, however, is neither the individual nor the church but that "all creation will be the Spirit-filled body of Christ." Accordingly, "the goal of the Pentecostal movement should be to put itself out of business"—for with the renewal of all things its mission is accomplished.

At the close of each of the chapters Jones speaks to relevant questions that people have raised (in talks given to Episcopal, Catholic, and Reformed church audiences). The reader will note a marked sensitivity to the concerns of various kinds of people—alienated, antagonistic, seeking, uncertain, etc.—and will appreciate the way the replies are given in a humble and straightforward manner. I commend this book without hesitation for those charismatically involved as a deeper and broader appreciation of their own experience. Also, as another reviewer, Morton Kelsey, has written, "There is no better book on the gifts of the Spirit to put into the hands of an inquiring clergyman or an intelligent layman."

Larry Christenson, a well-known Lutheran pastor and charismatic leader, has just written two very helpful books. (He has been known for many years for his *Speaking in Tongues* and *The Christian Family*.) The first, entitled *A Message to the Charismatic Movement* (Minneapolis: Bethany, 1972), carries as its basic theme that however much the church needs the charismatic movement, it is also true that the movement needs the church: its structure and order. In this short book Christenson treats some of the history of the little known Catholic Apostolic Church (which grew out of the ministry of Edward Irving, a Presbyterian churchman of the early 19th century) which had no conflict between charism and hierarchy. The story of this church is fascinating, and especially as a precursor of the contemporary charismatic scene. The second book, *A Charismatic Approach to Social Action* (Minneapolis: Bethany, 1974), is an important attempt to show how charismatic vitality is related to the social dimensions of Christianity. One of the frequent criticisms of the contemporary renewal is that it is essentially unrelated to social questions. Christenson seeks to parry this criticism by showing that the basic question is not *whether* we are to get involved in social action but *where* and *how*. One of Christenson's interesting points is his statement that the world does not write the agenda—as social activism often says—but it is the Lord himself who summons to particular actions: "A charismatic approach to social action does not set out to reform society. Its concern is to remain responsive and obedient to the Lord . . . serving in that place which he has pointed out."

Next I turn to a beautiful book by Robert Frost, *Set My Spirit Free* (Plainfield, N.J.: Logos, 1973). Earlier books by Dr. Frost, such as *Aglow with the Spirit* and *Overflowing Life,* have influenced countless numbers of people in discovering the deeper experience of "baptism in the Spirit" and the life abundant that flows out of it. In *Set My Spirit Free,* Frost (now professor of Spiritual Foundations at Melodyland School of Theology in Anaheim, California) discusses at length the role of the Holy Spirit in the liberation of our lives.

The writing throughout is an extraordinary combination of personal testimony, scientific analysis (his Ph.D. is in the field of biology), and wise spiritual counsel. The whole book intends to point a way of showing how people may be restored to a place of spiritual health and vitality. Robert Frost writes with the lyrical flow and nuance of a born poet. I commend this book highly.

A large number of charismatic books of an autobiographical nature have recently appeared. I will mention three of them written from within different traditions. Michael Harper, an Anglican priest, in his book *None Can Guess* (London: Hodder and Stoughton, 1971), recounts in a fascinating manner the story of his own spiritual renewal in 1962 and how this has led, through the establishment of Fountain Trust in England, to a ministry of assisting churches of all denominations to understand and experience the life of the Spirit and charismatic manifestations. *The Gift Is Already Yours* (Plainfield, N.J.: Logos, 1973), written by Lutheran pastor Erwin Prange, recounts the frustrating struggle of serving in a Brooklyn parish for many years until the day when he cried: "God, you and I are going to have it out right now. Either you are going to become real, or I am going to give up this farce!" Then came the answer: "The gift is already yours. Reach out and take it." The account that follows is one of high adventure as the church catches fire and Prange moves toward spiritual maturity in the years that follow. The last book I would mention is entitled *Clap Your Hands!* (Plainfield, N.J.: Logos, 1973) by Larry Tomczak, a young Catholic layman. This is the delightful and moving story of growing up in a Polish Catholic family and the struggle young Larry went through in finding a living relationship with Christ and a new dimension of power in the Holy Spirit. A born leader (rock band for years, student body president at Cleveland State University, then a member of the AFL-CIO headquarters staff in Washington), Tomczak at age 24 has now gone into full-time Christian service as an evangelist. The story is very well written and will be of particular interest for the Catholic reader.

Finally, I conclude with mentioning a small paperback entitled *In God's Providence: The Birth of a Catholic Charismatic Parish* (Plainfield, N.J.: Logos, 1973) by Fr. John Randall. Fr. Randall, a leader of the Catholic charismatic renewal in New England, writes from the background of biblical scholarship (doctorate in theology from Louvain) and from experience as a former spiritual director in the Cursillo Movement. Since his participation in the charismatic experience (which he vividly describes), there has been an extraordinary renewal over the last five years of St. Patrick's parish in Providence, Rhode Island. The description of this renewal concludes with the words: "What God the Father wants to do in our time is to build up in every city and in every town a body of his Son, a whole body, where people can come and see Jesus Christ . . . reach out and touch him, just as the crowd of Galilee did. This is what's happening. This is total renewal of his Church by God himself. Praise him!" This last little book is "must" reading for anyone who wishes a deeper sense of what the charismatic movement is all about.

TONGUES **Sister Maura**

It is the eve of Pentecost. Wherever the room was, it is here. Whoever waited and prayed, prays and waits.

In the invalid bed, the old woman breathes tongues; loud, unclear.
One who watches hears the groaning gates.

Her tongues batter the world she knows: this room with its gatherings:
commode, air cushion, dark bottles, needle, spoons.

Her tongues speak: the patch where an eye had been, the film of
glaucoma, terrible trembling hands the clatter

at bells and cups, the raucous voice bellowing from broken lungs,
the bony body thrusting to debate

with silence. Who hears the tongues? Who dare not hear? Each receives a language absolutely his alone.

Tongues, palpable, not on fire. If you listen, you will hear. If you dare not, take even greater care.

Sister Maura, S.S.N.D. is professor of English at the College of Notre Dame of Maryland and the author of six collections of poetry. Her latest book of poem-meditations is *Walking on Water* (Paulist Press).

ADULT EDUCATION PROGRAM

by Bernadette Kenny and Robert Heyer

GENERAL INTRODUCTION

The purpose of this educational supplement is to provide a practical plan for adult religious education. This plan will be based on selected articles from each issue of NEW CATHOLIC WORLD and will provide adult education programs for eight weeks.
Each session will be built upon key articles and will explose outward from these experiences, information, and group techniques.

The NEW CATHOLIC WORLD ADULT EDUCATION PROGRAM provides:
—continuous preplanned adult education program
—rich range of topics
—short-term commitment
—CCD teacher-enrichment program
—probing content-articles on today's issues integrated with experience-centered educational plans
—educational tools that are practical and spark interest

The creation of a climate conducive to learning is very important. A proper climate in an educational setting should help people be at ease and should stimulate sharing as well as personal activity. Clear, concise directions and careful preparation will facilitate this. Therefore:
—the director should prepare carefully beforehand.
—participants should have read the related articles.
—if a series of directions are given the director should wait until one stage is completed before announcing the next stage.
—the purpose of each session as well as its relation to the whole should be explained.

I. FIRST WEEK PROGRAM (90 Minutes) WHO IS THE CHARISMATIC?

A. INTRODUCTION

—The aim of this session is to understand the nature of the charismatic movement in the Catholic Church.
—Participants should have read Cohen's and Martin's articles.
—Materials: copies of the discussion questions for each small group.

B. EDUCATIONAL PLAN

(5 Minutes)

1. Director introduces aim of session, emphasizing that both Martin and Cohen provide an inside view of the charismatic Church. The discussion questions are based on both of these articles. (10 Minutes)
2. Divide the participants into groups of 5-6. Allow a few minutes to become acquainted and to select a recorder for each group. (5 Minutes)
3. Distribute copies of the six questions based on Cohen and Martin to each group. The task of each group is to reflect on and discuss the questions.

(30 Minutes)
Questions for Discussion:

a. What does the charismatic experience mean for individuals?
b. What does it mean for the Church?
c. What does it mean for Christianity?
d. What does it mean for society at large?
e. What is the relationship between the charismatics and the Churches?
f. What are some authentic signs of the work of the Spirit in the Church?

4. Each group then draws up three questions about the nature of the charismatic movement.
(5 Minutes)
5. Each group joins one other group and the members of each group try to answer the other group's questions.
(20 Minutes)
6. One person from each double group then summarizes for all the participants how the group sees the nature of the charismatic movement.
(5 Minutes)
7. Each group joins one other group and the members of each group try to answer the other group's questions.
(20 Minutes)
8. One person from each double group then summarizes for all the participants how the group sees the nature of the charismatic movement.
(15 Minutes)
9. Director concludes with a prayer that the participants may be able to listen to the movement of the Spirit in today's Church.

II. SECOND WEEK PROGRAM (90 Minutes) CHARISMATICS AND THE PARISH

A. INTRODUCTION

—The purpose of this session is to understand the relationship between the charismatic Church and the local parish.

—Participants should have read Ferry's article.

—Before this session the director asks three people to each speak on one of the areas in which parishes are experiencing problems today: 1. prayer; 2. social involvement; 3. community. The point of these talks is not to deny accusations but to highlight the problem and to give examples of how this problem is experienced in the local parish.

B. EDUCATIONAL PLAN

1. Director explains purpose of the session and introduces the three speakers.
(5 Minutes)
2. Each speaker gives short talk.
(15 Minutes)
3. Divide the participants into small groups of 6-8 people. Allow a few minutes for introductions and choosing of a recorder.
4. The task of each group is to draw up a list of ways that the charismatics may contribute to a solution to each of these problem areas.
(40 Minutes)
5. The recorder from each group

summarizes the group's discussion for the other participants. (15 Minutes)

6. The director either asks for suggestions from the participants or gives some suggestions himself about how this local parish may go about meeting the three needs of prayer, social involvement and community. (10 Minutes)
7. Director concludes with a prayer for help in meeting these needs.

III. THIRD WEEK (90 Minutes)
CHARISMATICS—A NEW RELIGIOUS ORDER?

A. INTRODUCTION

—The purpose of this session is to compare the charismatic movements with the old religious orders in the Church.

—Participants should have read Malone's article.

—Materials: Newsprint large enough for a group to work on; magic markers.

B. EDUCATIONAL PLAN

1. Director introduces the session, explaining its purpose. (5 Minutes)
2. Divide participants into small groups of 6-8 people. Distribute a large sheet of newsprint and magic markers to each group. (5 Minutes)
3. The task of each group is to brainstorm for characteristics of the pre-Vatican II religious orders. These should be written on the left hand side of the newsprint. (20 Minutes)
4. Using Malone's article as a reference, each group now brainstorms for characteristics of the charismatics at Ignatius House. These should be written on the right-hand side of the newsprint. (20 Minutes)
5. Each group chooses a recorder and discusses the question: In what ways can the charismatics be considered a new religious order? (20 Minutes)
6. Recorder summarizes the group's discussion for all the participants. (20 Minutes)
7. Director concludes with a prayer asking that in our attempts to be a faith community, we do not become narrow-minded or exclusive.

IV. FOURTH WEEK PROGRAM (90 Minutes) THE SOCIAL SCIENTISTS' VIEW

A. INTRODUCTION

—The aim of this session is to take a look at the charismatic movement, using the tools of the social scientist.

—Participants should have read Fichter's article.

—Before the session, director asks four people to be members of a panel.

B. EDUCATIONAL PLAN

1. Director explains aim of session and introduces panel members. (5 Minutes)
2. Each panel member summarizes and comments on one of the surprises that sociologists have encountered in the charismatic movement. Each panelist should also say how in his judgment he sees this as good or bad. (25 Minutes)
3. Director or one of the participants presents Fichter's critique of the charismatic approach to women and to social justice. (10 Minutes)
4. The task of the small groups is to discuss the question: "On the face of the evidence, can the charismatic movement be considered a traditionalist movement in the Church?" (20 Minutes)
5. Recorder reports the group's conclusions for all the participants. (20 Minutes)
6. Director concludes with a prayer.

V. FIFTH WEEK PROGRAM (90 Minutes) SPIRIT AND INSTITUTION

A. INTRODUCTION

—The aim of this session is to understand the relationship between the charismatics and the institutional Church.

—Participants should have read Gelpi's article.

—Materials: Paper and crayons or magic markers.

B. EDUCATIONAL PLAN

1. Director introduces aim of session. He links this to the second week program by saying that this week's session picks up where the second session left off. (5 Minutes)
2. Director asks a number of participants to call out the first word that comes to their minds when they hear the word charismatic. These are written on a chalkboard.
3. Director asks a number of people to call out the first word that comes to their minds when they hear the term institutional Church. These should be written on a chalkboard. (20 Minutes)
4. Divide people into small groups. Allow a few minutes for introductions and selection of a recorder. (5 Minutes)
5. The task of the small groups is to discuss the question: "What can the charismatics and the institutional Church offer each other?" (20 Minutes)
6. The recorder from each group reports back for all the participants. (15 Minutes)
7. Each small group then prepares a drawing to profile a Spirit-filled member of the hierarchy and a truly Christian community as described by Gelpi. (10 Minutes)
8. These may be taped around the room and one person from each group comments on them. (10 Minutes)
9. Director concludes with a prayer that the participants may grow as a Christian community.

VI. SIXTH WEEK (90 Minutes) DAILY LIFE IN THE SPIRIT

A. INTRODUCTION

—The aim of this session is to see the gifts of the Spirit as operative in the New Testament and then to see how they operate in our lives today.

—Materials: New Testament (at least one for each small group); a list of the gifts of the Spirit either on chalkboard or overhead transparency: Wisdom, Understanding, Knowledge, Counsel, Fortitude, Piety, Fear of the Lord.

B. EDUCATIONAL PLAN

1. Director introduces the session and explains the purpose. He may also wish to say a few words about each gift.
   (10 Minutes)
2. Divide participants into small groups of 6-8 people. Each group will choose one of the gifts of the Spirit and research the New Testament for examples of that gift in action. The following texts might be helpful in the search: Mt. 26:36-40; Mt. 26:57-68; Lk. 9:23-27; Lk. 15:4-7; Lk. 11:38-42; Lk. 11:9-13; Lk. 12:22-32; Lk. 21:1-4; Mt. 20:20-23.
   (30 Minutes)
3. Each group will then take one of the texts that demonstrates its gift and prepare to role-play a contemporary version of that account.
   (20 Minutes)
4. Each group role-plays its text.
   (15 Minutes)
5. The director invites comments from the participants on how they see the gifts of the Spirit in everyday life.
   (10 Minutes)
6. Director concludes with a prayer such as "Come, Holy Spirit" or a reading from 1 Corinthians 12:3-7 and 12-13.

VII. SEVENTH WEEK PROGRAM (90 Minutes) INNER HEALING

A. INTRODUCTION

—The purpose of this session is to understand Scanlon's message about the healing power of the Lord.

—Participants should have read Scanlon's book, *Inner* Healing (Paulist Press).

B. EDUCATIONAL PLAN

1. Director introduces purpose of session.
2. Director lists Scanlon's distinctions in knowing how to minister the healing power of the Lord. He also comments on them.
   (10 Minutes)
3. Participants divide into small groups. Allow a few minutes for introductions and choosing a recorder.
   (5 Minutes)
4. The task of the small groups is to discuss Scanlon's three distinctions and to list several examples from their own experience of each of these.
   a. The distinction between those whose faith is strong enough to face painful memories and those who cannot do this.
   b. The distinction between root

memories and surface memories.

c. The distinction between specific memories and general memories.
(20 Minutes)

5. Recorder reports group's list to all participants.
(15 Minutes)

6. Each small group then prepares to role-play a scene in which healing is needed.
(15 Minutes)

7. Small groups perform role-playing and director invites comments from all the participants.
(20 Minutes)

8. Director concludes with a prayer asking that participants may have "new hearts and new spirits."

VIII. EIGHTH WEEK (90 Minutes) LITURGY CELEBRATING THE SPIRIT

A. INTRODUCTION

—This entire session will be a liturgy celebrating the presence of the Spirit in our lives.

B. LITURGY OF THE WORD

1. Preparation
Select a small group and prepare them to do the entrance introduction.

2. Entrance Rite
Celebrant invites the community to listen to a conversation on the need for more quiet reflection in our busy life with words such as:
Let us listen for a moment
to a typical conversation on
our need for quiet reflection.
Four prepared members of the community, standing in a semicircle facing the community. begin a brief conversation. It goes as follows:

a. One after another, each expresses two comemnts on the need for quiet reflection in this busy, noisy, everyday life. N.B. Each comment goes in clear order: 1, 2, 3, 4—not all at once.

b. The first speaker's third comment goes off the topic. He speaks about last night's sports event on TV.

c. The second speaker's third comment is on another topic, e.g., the problem of busing and education.

d. The third speaker, with his third comment, begins another tangential topic, e.g., buying a new house.

e. The fourth speaker with his third comment begins a fourth tangential conversation by commenting about his new job.

f. The first speaker's fourth comment is on the TV show. The second speaker's fourth comment is on the problem of busing. The third speaker's fourth comment is on his new house. The fourth speaker's fourth comment is on his new job.

g. The first speaker brings back the conversation to the main topic. This is followed by comments on the main topic by one or two others.

h. During the unified conversation, the eyes and attention of the speakers should be visibly oriented to listening to one another. During the disparate comments they should not have eye contact and disunity should be visible.

i. This can be done briefly and powerfully without too much preparation.

3. Penance Rite
Litany Response: We beg your forgiveness, O Lord.
. . . For failing to listen to persons.
. . . For prejudging others too quickly.
. . . For our lack of openness in receiving others.
. . . For pushing through everyday life separated from per-
. . . sonal contact with Christ.
. . . For our indifferent and impersonal approach to new persons we meet.
. . . For so often giving only lip service.

4. Call to Worship
Lord our Creator,
you have blessed us with
language and understanding.
But we have become a babbling
people, searching little,
listening less.
Our understanding has been
dulled.
Send over us your Spirit, Lord,
that we may learn silence again,
that our words may become
sensitive with authentic
meaning.
Send your Spirit that we may
sing your praise in silence
and in song.

5. Readings Acts 2:1-11
Verse:
Send forth your Spirit and they will be created and you will renew the face of the earth.
Response:
Alleluia. Come, Holy Spirit, fill the hearts of your faithful; and kindle in them the fire of your love.
Verse:
Alleluia. In various tongues the apostles told of the wonderful works of God.
Response:
Alleluia. Come, Holy Spirit. . . .
Verse:
The Holy Spirit will teach you everything I have said to you.
Response:
Alleluia. Come, Holy Spirit. . . .
Verse:
I leave you peace, alleluia; I give you my peace.
Response:
Alleluia. Come, Holy Spirit. . . .
Verse:
Alleluia. It is the Spirit who gives life; the flesh profits nothing.
Response:
Alleluia. Come, Holy Spirit. . . .
Gospel
John 20:19-23
Petitions
Response: O Lord, send your Spirit!
1: That we may understand ourselves and the signs you write in our lives.
2: That wisdom may become alive in us.
3: That the gift of counsel may aid us in listening, giving your word of life.
4: That we may grow in fortitude of faith, in letting faith live in our daily decisions.
5: That authentic fear of the Lord may nourish our piety.